The Secret Place

Becoming the Apple of God's Eye

Jackeline Alfonzo

The Secret Place: *Becoming the Apple of God's Eye* By Jackeline Alfonzo

© 2022 Jackeline Alfonzo

Printed in the United States of America

ISBN: 9798847899062

Cover design, photographs and graphics: Jackeline Alfonzo

For invitations and conferences: jackeline.alfonzo@gmail.com
Instagram: Jackeline_lovefaith
Twitter: jackelinealfon1

All rights reserved solely by the author. The author guarantees all contents are original and do not infringe upon the legal rights of any other person or work. No part of this book may be reproduced, stored in a retrieval system, or transmitted in any form or by any means without expressed written permission of the author.

All quotes, unless otherwise noted, are from the New King James Version. Copyright 1979, 1980, 1982 by Thomas Nelson, Inc. Used by permission. All rights reserved.

Scriptures marked NIV are taken from the HOLY BIBLE, NEW INTERNATIONAL VERSION,. Copyright © 1973, 1978, 1984 by International Bible Society. Used by permission of Zondervan Publishing House. All rights reserved.

Scriptures marked KJV are taken from The Holy Bible, King James Version. Copyright © 1972 by Thomas Nelson Inc., Camden, New Jersey 08103.

Scripture marked MSG are taken from The Message. Published by permission. Originally published by NavPress in English as THE MESSAGE: The Bible in Contemporary Language copyright 2002 by Eugene Peterson. All rights reserved.

Scriptures marked NLT are taken from the Holy Bible, New Living Translation, copyright © 1996, 2004, 2007 by Tyndale House Foundation. Used by permission of Tyndale House Publishers, Inc., Carol Stream, Illinois 60188. All rights reserved.

Dedication

This book is dedicated to those who grew up dreaming of a better life, but lost hope. Believe in God, believe in yourself.

> *"Did I not say to you that if you would believe you would see the glory of God?"*
>
> —Jesus Christ

Acknowledgements

Thank you to the love of my life, **my LORD**, the God who sees, the God who listens, the God who remembers, the God who is faithful, the God who is real, and the God who opens ways where there are no ways. Thank you **my LORD** for always believing in me when others did not.

Thank you **Jesus Christ** because you were looking for me, you found me, you rescued me, and you saved me from the slavery and death of sin to give me abundant life.

Thank you Holy Spirit because without **YOU**, I would not have been able to write this book.

The following is a list of all the people I am grateful to, including my beloved mother Geovanina and father Alexis, my sisters and brothers, in-laws, nephews, nieces, aunts, uncles, and cousins. I wish to express my sincere gratitude to my two dear grandmothers and aunt who are in heaven. God has blessed me with all of you who are part of my imperfect-perfect family. I have been motivated and taught by you.

Thank you to my friends and to each person who has been a bridge for me to advance to the next stage of my life. Your presence has been very valuable in my life.

Thank you to all my professors from my ESOL classes for your dedication, and for encouraging every student to grow beyond their limitations. This book is proof of that.

Thanks to my mentor and editor of the first version, Dawn Owens, The Corporate Couch, for give me the opportunity to write this book.. Although you knew it would be challenging, you still trusted me.

My thanks go out to every pastor and every person who taught me in every church, and I am thankful to God for bringing them to me where I served. You deepened my relationship with God, made me more loving, and answered hundreds of questions I had about life, God, and why suffering occurs. Finally, I would like to thank everyone who prayed for me in order to accomplish God's perfect plan in my life.

Introduction

"And behold, I am coming quickly, and My reward is with Me, to give to every one according to his work. I am the Alpha and the Omega, the Beginning and the End, the First and the Last."

—Jesus Christ

"I desire mercy, and not sacrifice; and the knowledge of God rather than burnt offerings."

—Hosea 6:6.

I am Jackeline Alfonzo, a woman who is totally in love with God and living for Him. My faith in Him is one of my main gifts. In 2009-2010 I started to thirst and hunger for The Word of God. I also had some questions about life and I wanted answers, so I began to read the Bible. Over time, I started to tell God that I wanted to know Him more, and that I wanted to attend church where I could be helped to know Him better. I'd gone as far as I could on my own, so I needed help to continue growing in His knowledge. One day, I had an encounter with God that was so vivid and so real, it completely changed my life. I was sitting in front of my work computer when a brief "video" of my entire life, flashed through my mind. Each one of those events were good acts of generosity, collaboration, charm, and love I had experienced with my family, friends, co-workers; even people I did not know but for whom I'd done something good. Some of those memories I had forgotten until that moment when they came to my mind again. I was seeing and hearing in a new and different way than I had before. God was opening my senses! That was the beginning of my new relationship with Him, as He started to show me the Truth of life and love.

I deeply believe that love is the most valuable and greatest gift that God has given us. However, people are losing the real meaning of love and mercy for them and others. The main reason is that they are disconnected from our Creator, our God. His greatest commandment says that we have to love Him with all our mind, soul, and heart, and the second says we have to love each other as we love ourselves. However, if we do not have a real relationship with God, if we do not seek Him, we are not able to really know and love Him as our Heavenly Father. As a result, people do not know how to love themselves nor love others because they are far away from the source, which is God.

I have written this book in hopes of sharing some important lessons with you regarding my family, career, and life as it relates to God working in me; and ultimately in us. My prayer is to impact the unbeliever. A part of that lesson relates to how COVID-19 is covering the earth, as it signals the warnings written in The Bible that Jesus is coming back again soon. God wants us to seek Him. He talks to each one of us every day, every second of our life, but we must be connected with Him. It is time to know God as Father, as Son, and as Holy Spirit. Then people will know the truth of Him. Jesus Christ said, "You will know the truth, and the truth will set you free." Part of that truth is who God says you are. You are what God says and not what society or other people say about you. That truth allows you to know how much God loves you. Consequently, you will really know how to love Him, how to love yourself, and how to love other people. That truth will help you stay stable in difficult moments because you are trusting in the Rock, Jesus Christ. That truth will let you know what real death is, and what your real salvation is about. We do not know when Jesus, the Son of God is coming, just like we do not know our own number of days to dwell upon this earth. Perhaps it is the same with the coming of Jesus Christ. This is even more true as God provides clear evidence of what the whole world is facing today. At it is written in 2 Peter 3:8-9, "for God, one day is like a thousand years, and a thousand years are like a day." He is not slow in keeping His promises. He wants everyone to come to repentance. He wants you to be saved because He loves you.

Table of Contents

Acknowledgements...v
Introduction vi

Chapter 1 11
    Family Ties

Chapter 2 20
    Love

Chapter 3 30
    Faith and Obedience

Chapter 4 41
    Wisdom and Identity

Chapter 5 53
    Death

Chapter 6 67
    Forgiveness

Chapter 7 77
    Process

Chapter 8 91
    Purpose

Chapter 9 105
    Salvation

Chapter 10 119
    Time

CHAPTER 1

Family Ties

> *"Vanity of vanities, all is vanity. What profit has a man from all his labor in which he toils under the sun?"*
>
> —*Ecclesiastes 1:2 (NKJV)*

My lovely Aunt Dai was a 56-year-old single woman who was born in Venezuela, in a small city called El Tigre. Dai was the only girl of the four children of my grandmother, who my siblings and I call "Abuelita", which is a Spanish word for "grandmother." Dai was my dad's sister. Some of her main characteristics were, grateful, worker, committed, brave, strong, passionate, happy, and she also was a dreamer. She had blessed hands to work and obtain outstanding results with all she used to do. She had a simple natural beauty; she was thin, with smooth, porcelain-like skin and deep brown eyes. Her laugh was amazing! When something made her laugh, the sound filled the room. Her life was short, but she left us valuable messages.

Although she did not have children, she was a sweet girl with the kids, especially with her nieces and nephews. My fondest memories of her include the holiday seasons.

For example, Christmas time was amazing. She used to prepare and cook with Abuelita, her adoptive sister, and my mother traditional

Christmas food, such hallacas and chicken salad with apples. Even though my brother and I were children, she allowed us to participate in the hallacas preparation. Those were loved moments, each time we were sitting at the back of Abuelita's home.

The summer was amazing also. Because Abuelita was born in Margarita island and her siblings and part of her family was there, she, Dai, Diose (who was like a sister for Abuelita), my brother Hito, and I used to travel to Margarita during our vacations in August. We stayed in Abuelita's mother's house, where my father was born. We used to go to parties and town festivities. Other days we visited some of the beautiful tourist places and Abuelita's friends. Most of the time, while we were waiting for Abuelita to say a final goodnight to her friends, Dai and Diose would tell my brother and me funny things to make us laugh. For example, she said, "Let's count how many times Tella (she used to call Abuelita by her nickname) says *ahora si me despido, hasta luego pues (goodnight this time is true, see you soon)*." Abuelita would keep talking until around 30 minutes after she'd said her original goodbye to her friends. Also, each night when we were ready to sleep, Dai started to remember all the funny anecdotes from the day, especially about Abuelita or Diose, so we all started to talk and laugh a lot. Abuelita, Dai, and Diose were so funny, happy, and lovely women, so Hito and I loved to travel or to spend time with them because they played and made us laugh a lot.

My beloved aunt had blessed hands. Every time that we visited my grandmother's house, Dai's bedroom was the preferred place for my brother and me to hang out. She had her closet filled with stuffed animals, most of which she made. She was amazing at making them and kept most of them all her life.

When Dai was 19 years old, she decided to move to Valencia (Venezuelan city) for new life opportunities. My grandmother had friends there whom she had worked with in El Tigre some years before, so they became like a family. Because of that, Dai was welcome in their home. She was another daughter to them. I clearly remember the night when my father, mother, brother, and I went with Dai to the bus terminal where she would leave for Valencia. There were lots of busses, smoke, people, and noise. She was on the bus, and we were standing near the bus talking with her through the window. My father was carrying me so I could hear her better. Then the driver sounded the horn to let people know that it was time to leave. I started to cry a lot because my dear aunt was leaving. So my father told her to call me immediately when she arrived at her new place. It was the first time I saw her departing.

In Valencia, she started a new life. She picked up different skills and talents. Her new passions included making/painting ceramics and knitting. She did all kinds of ceramics. Additionally, she knitted baby booties, baby hats, mini tablecloths, and blouses. I remember when one of my sisters was born, Dai gifted my mother a spectacularly decorated shoes box filled with a variety of colorful baby booties and hats. It was really awesome and beautiful. Even though my sister was not her blood niece, she was kind to prepare that for her. It was the same love with my two next sisters who were born later. She loved each one of them as her blood nieces.

Then she began a new undertaking. She and Abuelita's friend opened a Child Care Center. They had no more than 20 kids. The kindergarten was well known because of the excellent work they did. The kids and their parents called Dai "Tata." Some of them were the best in their schools because Dai taught the alphabet, numbers, and other lessons earlier. Eventually, Dai invited my brother and me to spend our vacation seasons with her, so we met the kids. They were sweet, beautiful, obedient, and quiet.

Dai used to travel to El Tigre during Easter Week and Christmas. We used to spend Easter Week in a small house of Abuelita located in a small town called La Canoa. It was the favorite place of the whole family, as well as friends and neighbors. Sometimes, there were as many as 15-20 people. It had a tiny mud house with two rooms. The kitchen was outside, and it was made of residual construction materials. As soon as we arrived there, Dai said, *"Bueno chamos vamos a trabajar. Primero, hay que hacer el bañito y limpiar el terreno,"* meaning, *"Well chamos (guys) let's work. First we have to do the small bathroom and clean the land."* A provisional restroom was done by Dai and her friends at the end of the ground, and all of us started to clear the land. Then, Dai joined us. We could spend almost two or three days cleaning it, but Dai was the one who really enjoyed doing it. She loved working with the land. While some were cleaning the grounds, others were cooking, sweeping, and organizing the small house. The children were flying kites and others played on the hammocks (chinchorros) made by Abuelita and Diose. We hung those amazing and relaxing chinchorros under a leafy tree that provided shade. It was the favorite place to sleep of Dai, my uncles, father, brother, and friends. Abuelita, my mother, the kids, and I used to sleep inside the small house.

The land did not have direct electricity, nor water. But it did have a radiant sun, a bright white moon, the sky full of stars, and an amazing river with a gentle stream.

The river and the small club were one of our diversions. All of us loved to be there, but we had to divide into groups in order to save all we had at the house. Because of the limitation of water and electricity, we used to be ready before sundown to go to the club. It was not comfortable to dress without light, so we used to take our showers early at the river. Then we went to the house to change our clothes, get ready to have dinner, and finally go to the club. Dai, her friends, my uncles, siblings, and I were ready to dance at the club.

Some days, Dai invited us to collect cashew seeds. La Canoa was replete of cashew trees, so Dai loved to collect and then to cook them. We used to gather a lot of seeds, and the job to prepare them was huge. Though the final number of cashews was few, we still enjoyed doing it with her. It was an amazing season of our life. We really enjoyed spending time there because it was a peaceful place. We could hear the sound of the birds in the sunset and throughout the morning, the bray of the donkeys at some specific hours, the voices and laughs of each one of us, or just listen to the silence. It was a simple place. Nothing there was fancy, but the family, friends, neighbors, the love, the jokes, the laughs, the peace, the sky, the day, the sun, the night, the moon, the stars, the river, the trees, the breeze, and the food made an immense difference.

> *"All streams flow into the sea, yet the sea is never full. To the place the streams come from, there they return again."*
>
> *—Ecclesiastes 1:7 (NIV)*

Like the rivers, after almost sixteen years, Dai came back to her mother, to her city. She loved being in Valencia, sharing with the family, working at the Child Care Center; however, she decided to return to take care of Abuelita, who was getting older, and her new baby niece who was born a few months before. It was part of her new job by that time. Also, Abuelita and she had rented three bedrooms of the house. One was Dai's bedroom. Since Abuelita's bedroom had space for one small bed, they were sharing it. The lease was mainly for students or singles; however, in a few cases, they rented to couples. Then when my cousin became a teenager, Dai was no longer taking care of her, so she needed to find another job.

Shortly afterward, she found a new occupation with something she loved. During the week, she had a part-time job in a peanut factory, in a farm, and in an organophonic. Dai loved planting. Every day, Dai woke up around 4:30 a.m. to prepare coffee and her food for the job. She would leave the lunch instructions to my sister, who worked taking care of my grandmother, wake up Abuelita at 6:00 a.m. to give her daily pills and coffee, and then go to work. She used to arrive home between 5 and 7 p.m. When I visited them, I used to sit with her in the TV room, and sometimes she fell asleep while we were talking and watching a program.

She sowed parsley, chives, eggplants, peppers, and so on. When I was working in Angola, she used to ask me for all kinds of seeds I found at the supermarkets. However, she got other seeds from drying those of the vegetables she had bought at the grocery. She was passionate about her job. Plenty of beautiful, aromatic, and fresh green parsley and chives, and big and radiant eggplants and peppers were some of her amazing and gorgeous harvest.

Sometime later, my brother bought some land where they used to spend their weekends. It was the favourite place of Dai, Abuelita, and my brother by that time. Dai used to call my brother every Thursday to say to him, *"Entonces vamos este sábado para el campo?"* (*"So, are we going to the land this Saturday?"*) She built two organoponics there. It had low-level concrete walls of 32.8 feet by 3.28 feet. Then she prepared the land, adding sow land, cattle dung, and earthworm liquid. She sowed there chili pepper, tomatoes, eggplants, and chives. Every Sunday, when they were almost ready to come back home, she said to my brother, *"Ayy, no me quiero ir para la casa, me quisiera quedar aquí."* (*"I really would not come back to home; I would like to stay here."*) Dai loved spending time in nature and working on her organophonics.

> *"The thief does not come except to steal, and to kill, and to destroy. I have come that they may have life, and that they may have it more abundantly."*
>
> —*John 10:10 NKJV*

My forever loved Aunt Dai might be considered a multifaceted active and happy woman, who loved each one of her nieces and nephews with all her heart. However, she faced difficult challenges and hard moments that were frustrating and turned her life upside down.

For example, Dai and her brothers loved one another, but when they grew up, differences started to appear. Their communication was not good.

She never got married, but I remember when I was a child, Dai had a boyfriend. She was around 15 or 16 years old. Her boyfriend was a tourist aircraft pilot who lived in the capital of Venezuela. He was Venezuelan and came from Italian parents. He used to visit her frequently. One day he gave us a beautiful, amazing, and loyal pure white Mucuchies dog. I did not know why Dai's relationship ended, and I did not ask her. Then, some years later, she met a person who wanted a relationship with her when she was in Valencia, but that also did not progress. Dai was a quiet woman. She loved to share with friends, but her relationships were not our main conversation. Some years later, she started another relationship, but he passed away suddenly.

Dai was a strong woman. She continued her life while working and sharing with my brother, father, my uncles, and some friends.

Even though renting the bedrooms was helping Abuelita and Dai to pay their bills, it was not healthy. She loved to clean, but it was not totally possible with a lot of people in the house. However, it was a way to get extra money. Sometimes, she used to complain a lot. The communication with my two uncles and father was affected by that situation. Dai was expecting more help from her brothers. For example, she wanted their help to paint the house or to do some job here and there. Sometimes it happened, but sometimes it did not. She had an extreme capacity for working and dedication to do things. So she was expecting the same from others. Then the barriers among them grew. It might have been extremely difficult for her to live with this opposition, but the difficult situation of Venezuela was another factor that affected her.

Dai had very good friends and neighbours who grew up with her in the same town. But she also shared with people who were not good friends. They were a bad influence on her. She was going out more, and even drinking more than usual. During weekends, she used to go out and drink. It was evident that her relationship with Abuelita and her brothers was deeply affected by this. She was loved by them, and they disagreed with that situation, but they did not manage it correctly. Their communication was offensive and confrontational. It was not appropriate. They started to hurt one another. However, God always protected her, and those people disappeared from her life.

My brother and I always wanted their reconciliation, and we found it when we used to meet to talk with them.

I could collaborate with her and Abuelita once I started to work in Egypt. I helped with the food, medicine, and care of my Abuelita. Also, I did pay my sister, depending on who was available and who did not have a job, to take care of my grandmother while Dai was working. At that time, they did not rent bedrooms anymore.

Dai hardly ever was sick. I remember she got a virus called chikungunya at the end of 2015. Then, in 2016, one day she was feeling something wrong in her belly. This was the same week when the Holy Spirit asked me to fast and pray for her and her brothers, and few months after a familiar meeting of reconciliation my brother and I organized. She was worried because she really felt a lot of pain in her belly. It was bigger and harder than normal. She had a medical test and needed a hysterectomy. Then, she contacted her almost-sister, who was a doctor in Valencia. Dai did not want to be operated on in El Tigre. She asked one of her brothers, with whom she had recently reconciled, to travel with her. He was the only person available to travel with her before her surgery. Then I arrived the day of the surgery. It was successful. The doctor showed me the big mass that was extracted. Dai was making great progress. Her post-surgery medical test results showed some minor issues related to her liver, but it did not look serious. She was taking her pills and medicines. Because she wanted to rest, she spent some months in Valencia. Then she came back home healthy and ready to continue her routine.

Everything was going well, but the separation between her, my uncles, and my father started again. I spoke to Dai about forgiving them, changing her mindset, and praying for them. However, she used to tell me that she did not want to forgive them.

Dai was in love with her job and other activities. She was our friend. She used to talk with us, all her nieces and nephews, like friends. She loved to cook for us. She was my best friend, who I used to call to tell her what I was facing in my job, or when something amazing was happening to me, or to ask her to pray for me when I needed it because she used to do it through the Bible. My brother told me that when they were talking, she used to tell him, "If someone tries to hurt my nieces and nephews, I will fight for them to protect them." She was like a purebred Mucuchies dog, loyal and brave for us. Additionally, she was my prayer squire, the person who prayed for me each time I needed it before I became a prayer intercessor. After that, I was her squire, and ever since I have been the squire of my family, friends, and each people, place, church, town, city, country, or any event that God assigns to me.

In June 2017, a little more than one year after her first surgery, I was in my apartment when she called me. She told me, *"Jacke, mija la barriga me esta creciendo otra vez." ("Jacke, my belly is growing again.")* When I heard that, I felt fear. I could not travel immediately, so one of my uncles used to call me to let me know that she had a lot of pain. My brother, father, and two uncles were helping her as they waited for me to arrive, and while we arranged everything needed for her travel and second surgery to be done in Valencia again.

This time it was impossible for her to travel by bus. My sister traveled with her by ambulance. By that time, the political situation in Venezuela was getting worse, so the streets were closed due to the protests. Additionally, because the ambulance was provided to us as a favor, we had to wait for the driver to deliver a packet in a city located in the opposite direction to Valencia, which made for a longer trip. I used to call my sister to ask how she was, and my sister told me that she was suffering because of some holes on the road the driver could not avoid, and also the ambulance was not comfortable. She arrived at the hospital at night after more than ten hours of traveling. Mari, the doctor, was waiting for her. She told me that when she saw Dai, she wanted to cry. Dai was totally pale and needed to recover her hemoglobin before the surgery, so a blood transfusion was needed. I arrived there that same week.

During the time she received the blood transfusion, my beloved aunt struggled to stay alive. One afternoon while I was buying some medicine, I received a call that she was not breathing well, and the nurses were giving her first aid. I immediately wrote to the Intercessor prayer team from the church to pray for her. I started to pray too. When I arrived in the bedroom, the nurses were still helping her, and I continued praying there. A few minutes later, she was stable.

The day of her surgery finally arrived. During the surgery, the doctor decided to do it in two parts because of Dai's condition. They needed to observe her reaction the next twenty-four hours. She did well, but was fighting to stay alive. The next day was the end of the surgery. It was successful; however, she was beginning to deteriorate and one of her legs was affected as a consequence of the cancer. She was not able to walk, so we had to stay at the hospital for her observation. With the treatment, prayer, and love, she recovered a few weeks after.

When I handed the biopsy results to the doctor, she told me "este es uno de los cánceres más agresivos que existe, pero aún la tendrás por un largo tiempo" (It is one of the most aggressive cancers, but you'll still have her for a long time).

The bedroom of that hospital was our bedroom for a little more than one month. But God always is good. Even though it was a public hospital, we were on a floor that had been renovated some months before. It was like a clinic floor, and the bedroom was comfortable with three beds. So during our time there, I always had a bed to sleep in. I assisted each patient in the room that needed help. I provided them with food, medicine, and prayer. God is faithful, and He never leaves us alone. He blesses us, so we must bless others.

CHAPTER 2

Love

"Love is seeing your loved one suffering,
and you are suffering with them.
Love is seeing your loved one crying,
and you are crying with them.
Love is seeing your loved one dying,
and you are dying with her.

Love is when you were a teenager, and you observed a young man at a distance running in the street with one of his hands on his bleeding head and the other carrying a bag of bread falling while he was running; so you feel helpless because you are far from him. Then when you arrived at home, and you were telling your mother, father, and grandmother what happened, you cry in the middle of the story because you remembered the boy protecting his head and trying to protect the bread inside the bag, but you were too far away to help him.

Love is when you stand in the middle of two of your loved ones while they were trying to hurt each other. It was not because you believe you are stronger or you do not care for your life but because your love for them is so big that you just wanted to save and protect them. Then, immediately, you can see the meaning of the love of Jesus Christ for us when He went to the cross."

—Jackeline Alfonzo

I grew up knowing Jesus Christ is the son of God, and He died on the cross. However, I did not know the real and deep meaning of what He did for us until 2015 when I started to attend the Christian Church. Isaiah 53 KJV: "³He is despised and rejected of men; a man of sorrows, and acquainted with grief: and we hid as it were our faces from him; He was despised, and we esteemed Him not. ⁴Surely He hath borne our griefs, and carried our sorrows: yet we did esteem him stricken, smitten of God, and afflicted." When I read Isaiah 53 the first time, it touched and penetrated my heart. I just cried each time I read it, and I became more grateful, committed, and in love with Jesus Christ.

> *"Love does not give up. Love is kind. Love is not jealous. Love does not put itself up as being important. Love has no pride. Love does not do the wrong thing. Love never thinks of itself. Love does not get angry. Love does not remember the suffering that comes from being hurt by someone. Love is not happy with sin. Love is happy with the truth."*
>
> *—1 Corinthians 13: 4-6 NLV*

The Scripture above expanded my vision of love and made me understand people better. For example, I define Abuelita, my grandmother, as Love. When I was a child, we used to visit her each afternoon. Her house had some ceramics as decoration. One of them was an orange flamingo with a long and thin neck. From the first moment I saw it, it called my attention, and I thought "I guess I have the strength to break the neck of the flamingo in two." It was not because I wanted to break it—my family says my brother and I were some of the quietest kids who existed—it was just because I was curious. So one day, I took the flamingo and I broke it. However, after I broke it, I was nervous and scared because Abuelita cared a lot about her things. Then I showed it to my mother, and she told me, *"Cuando tu abuela regrese del trabajo Ud. le muestra la ceramica."* ("When your grandma comes from the job, show her the ceramic.") I was totally nervous waiting for her. Then, when she arrived, I showed her the broken flamingo. She was calm and quiet. She just told me, *"Do not to do it again; you just always toque con los ojos y mira con las manos"* (touch with your eyes, and see with your hands). So with her reaction, she showed me how much she loved me. She did not know it, but I kept that moment in my heart. I am sure my mother knew ahead of the reaction of Abuelita, but she also wanted to teach me to be a careful and responsible kid.

> *"My people are destroyed for lack of knowledge."*
>
> *—Hosea 4:6 KJV*

Hosea 4:6 was one of the first verses the Holy Spirit gave me when I became a pure Christian. However, since early in my life, it has been very important to act in the right way. When I detect I am doing something wrong, I stop and correct it. God started His job with me regarding love a long time ago. My family was my first school. I have some testimonies:

When I was at the university, I traveled to visit my family just two times per year. One day, I noticed that every time I arrived, my two younger sisters would ask me, "When are you leaving?" I did not know why they asked me that until one day when I did something mean to my sister Key. I asked her to prepare a fruit juice. She did not want to make it. However, I continued asking for it, and she prepared it. I was expecting a delicious juice as she used to prepare, but she made just a water of juice because she did not want to obey. Then I took the jar and poured the juice on her head. I remember clearly when she started crying and asked me, *"¿Por qué me hiciste eso Jacke?"* ("Why did you do it to me, Jacke?") Her eyes crying broke my heart. From that moment, I started to reflect on how I was treating my two loved sisters. I asked myself, *"¿Qué estoy haciendo? (What am I doing?) I do not want my sisters to feel afraid of me. I want them to respect and love me."* So immediately I started to rectify myself. They were my two loved little sisters, who I used to take care of for some hours every morning when my mother went to work. Also, I used to take them for a walk some afternoons. I deeply love them. My intention was not to hurt them ever, but I was doing it unconsciously.

My mother's mom, who we calle Mamá, was different than Abuelita. Mamá was more serious, and she was not as sweet as Abuelita. Also, she used to complain sometimes. When my brother and I used to come back to her home after we spent the weekend in Abuelita's house, Mamá would be upset. When we asked the blessing, she would not answer us. Her answer was important to us, but she kept silent. We grew up with the tradition of asking the blessing of our older family. It is important for us. Every day when we wake up, the first time we see an elder of our family, when we are going to sleep, or saying goodbye after a visit, we ask them "bendición," a hug and kiss on the cheek or forehead to our mother, grandmother, father, uncles, aunts, and among the older siblings and cousins. It has been for generations, from my father's family and my mother's family. So when she did not give us her blessing, I used to think she did not love us. My brother and I grew up feeling scared and distant from her. But I was more distant because of her strong character and face. Then when I grew up, I understood she was jealous, and it was her way of reacting.

One night my aunt (my mother's twin sister) told me, *"Jacke acercate a Mamá mija." (Jacke, come closer to Mamá mija.) "Do not be afraid of her."* So from that moment, I started to be closer to Mamá, and my relationship with her improved a lot. I started to do for her the same as I was doing with Abuelita. When I bought a present for Abuelita, I did the same for her. During my vacations with my family, I wanted to share my time with them all. So when I visited Abuelita, I used to take Mamá with me. Also, I used to spend some weekends with her, and we talked more. As a result, I found the loveliest grandmother in the world. I realized she was a sweet woman, with a sweet heart hidden behind a hard face. She was filled with love. She was a very helpful and serviceable woman who was a nurse almost all her life. She was a brave woman who used to live alone in difficult villages or towns far away from her family because she was the nurse there. Even though she showed strong character with my mother, she moved to the same zones where my mother was moving every time my mother did. With Mamá, I could see how a person who was a strong woman with a strong character could become a child as she was getting older.

She loved to dance with her grandsons. Each Christmas and New Year, she was ready to dance. She used to celebrate the New Year with us in my mother's house. So each December 31, she used to arrive at my mother's house around 7 or 8 p.m. She danced with my brother and cousins. Then she sat on the couch to remember each one of her daughters and sons. They lived in other cities. She had 12 children. One of them died when she was born and just four were living near her.

One day she had an unexpected stroke, and she died two days after it. When she passed away, I had one regret. I never told her that I loved her. From my mouth, she never heard how much I loved her. Even though I demonstrated it to her, I did not tell her. Not because I did not want to, but because I did not know how important it was that we must show our love but also say how much we love our loved ones.

After her funeral, I came back to Maracaibo, the city where I was working at that moment. Every day I was missing her more. One night, I woke up desperate and crying, dreaming that I did not tell her about my love for her. Then the next day I called Abuelita to tell her how much I loved her. I told her that I did not tell it to Mamá, but I was calling her to tell her that I loved her. Abuelita told me, *"Yo se mija, yo se que tú me amas y doña María también sabía que tú la amabas."* *("I know mija, I know you love me, and doña Maria also knew that you loved her.")*

Each December 31, the couch where Mamá used to sit was empty. We missed her sitting there waiting for the New Year and remembering, crying, and praying for her other daughters and sons, who were far away from her.

"It is only with the heart that we can see rightly; what is essential is invisible to the eye." This is a phrase from the book *The Little Prince* that touched my heart. Yes. God has taught me that with our hearts, we can see what is inside the other person. However, to do that, our hearts ought to be totally clean. Faith, love, and patience are needed to see with our heart's eyes. We can see with our hearts when we spend time with God, but also when we spend time with people. For that we have to go out of our comfort zones and give our love and our time. To see with our hearts, we have to stand in the place of the other person. If you see a strong face or body language saying something different from love, you have to see deeper inside. We do not know what that person might be living or would have lived. For example, Mamá and Dai were kind women who had a difficult life; they had a self-protection barrier created because they did not know the truth of life. Their daily challenges were taking from them their joy. Even when they believed in God, it was not enough. Spending time in His presence, to really know Him, was needed.

> *"And David said, is there anyone still left of the house of Saul to whom I can show kindness for Jonathan's sake?"*
>
> —*2 Samuel 9:1 NIV*

Loyalty, fidelity, and love existed between David and Jonathan since the first moment they met. They were not blood brothers, but they loved as brothers and they protected each other.

Dai was deeply loved by Abuelita and her three brothers. When I asked each one of them their best memories among them, they answered:

"I remember when Enriq, Dai, our neighbors and I played metras (marbles), and we spent all day playing in the backyard. Our house was the house of parties with all our neighbors, everybody was there. Also we all used to visit our aunts and cousins to play with them, and we spent one week there," said my uncle Will, the youngest one.

"I loved to spend time with Dai. We just have to know how to treat her, but I loved being with her, and I loved to share and spend time with Will, too. I remember when we had a football game in Margarita and we met Alex (brother). He attended to us. He was very kind with the football team, and he gave us food," said my uncle Enriq.

"Well, when I was eleven years old, two months, and 20 days, Enriq was born. I had to take care of him, but at my school time, I used to leave him in our neighbor's house while I was at the school," said my father.

Regarding Dai, "I asked '¿Te busta chiti?' I used to call her chiti. 'Estaba monísimo con mi hermanita.' ("I was so happy with my little sister.") I used to feed her, and she ate it. I asked her, '¿te busta chiti?' ("Do you like it, chiti?") I was showing my love for her," said my father Alex.

Dai was the apple of the eyes of her brothers, she was the apple of the eyes of Abuelita; she was deeply loved even by Abuelita's family and neighbours.

However, when, how, and why was that gorgeous relationship between Dai and her brothers broken? Who told them that they did not love one another? It might be that too much noise, not enough appropriate communication among them, and not spending time with

God was filling them with the wrong seeds. Mathew 13:24-26 talks about the good seed, and the tares that were sowed while the men were sleeping. God is the first who must be in a family, otherwise that strong foundation that initially was built will be fractured by a lot of external factors. To avoid this, the family ought to know the wisdom written in the Word of God. They as family must meditate on it, and they must pray according to the Word of God every day. The families must build the wall of prayer to protect themselves and their homes. They must avoid the lies and noise of life because it makes them forget the love among them.

In the Bible, Mephibosheth, the son of Jonathan, was lame of his feet because his nurse let him fall while they were trying to escape after Jonathan and Saul had died (2 Samuel 4:4). When my father was a teenager, he was attacked by an aggressive dog while he was carrying Enriq, his brother. He said that even though it was very difficult for the owners of that aggressive dog to remove her from my father, he kept his little brother in his arm. "It was a very difficult moment, and I was hurt and bitten a lot by the dog, pero no solté a mi hermano (but I did not drop my brother), and I kept him with me always," he told me. Like David and Jonathan protected each other, these siblings had love between them.

Real love cannot be hidden. I saw love among the siblings even when they thought their relationship was over. They helped one another through difficult situations, no matter what obstacles appeared in the "natural" realm. We can see and we can hear it with our spiritual senses connected with God Father, Jesus Christ, and the Holy Spirit through having a clean heart. Do not wait until the last moment to show your love to your family and the people around you. Psalm 133 says "...how good and pleasant it is for brethren to live in harmony and unity because the Lord God sends His blessings there." Do not lose your blessings.

Love is to share with others what we have even when we do not have a lot. We can do it when we have love and faith in God. Hebrews 10:24 KJV says: "And let us consider one another to provoke unto love and to good works." We must not feel scared to give to or share with others what we have because when we do it, we are sowing for ourselves and for future generations. So, if when we share or give to others, we are sowing for us and future generations, why don't we choose to give and share the best of us? For example, Abuelita was an immensely generous person. She worked in the passenger terminal of El Tigre city for a long time. I remember when Abuelita used to arrive home with someone who missed the bus or had to wait for the next bus the next day. Her house was a house for everybody she could help. Abuelita loved to talk with people. I imagine that she started conversations with those people whom she invited to sleep in her house. She did it a lot. Also, most of the time, she shared her food with her neighbors, or with whoever needed it. I remember her sending them some of her delicious soup or other special plate, and we would be the last to eat. She always had in her house something to give to the people even if it was a bath soap bar. She had the blessing of half a benefit food card. There was plenty of food. However, even though that blessing stopped one day, the food never ever was missed in her house. And she still gave to people what she could without fear. The Scripture says in Acts 20:35 that it is more blessed to give than to receive. I learned that of my loved Abuelita, and I am thankful for that. She fed my mother, brother, and me when my father was not with us. She did it also with my other sisters.

She was so cute when she became older. When some of her friends, families, or my siblings and I used to visit her, she would say, *"Ayy mija ni tengo nada que darles, ni un jaboncito tengo para darles."* (*"Ayy mija, I do not have anything to give you, not even a little soap bar to give you."*) We would just hug her and tell her each time that, *"Abuelita con su amor es suficiente, ya Ud. nos dió bastante, ahora nos toca a nosostros darle."* (*"Abuelita, your love is enough. You gave us a lot before and now it is our turn to give to you."*) And yes, it was our turn. My siblings and I did it every time. Each one of us returned to her the love she gave us. God blessed me by giving me the opportunity to care for Abuelita by providing medicines, care, food, cakes, flowers, gifts, travels, kisses, hugs, love, time, and more until the last day of her life. Nothing was too much.

Love is honoring our parents. Exodus 20:12 says that we have to honor our fathers and our mothers. I have been doing it, and I can see the blessings of God. My mother is a quiet and kind woman who did everything for my siblings and me when we were studying. When she did not have money to pay our studies, she sold all her gold rings that she had bought when she was working. So this was in my mind and heart; I grew up dreaming about a better life for her and my siblings.

It was my motivation. I wanted to give her a house with all that she needed. And God blessed me to be able to do that. My brother, sisters, and I honor her all the time. I know that when she is older, my nephews and nieces will give love just the same because she is like my two grandmothers were. Her house is our favorite place. It is amazing when all of us are with her in the kitchen. And her food is the best.

Even though I love my father, I did not know that I had to honor him. My brother and I did not grow up with him because my parents divorced when we were around 9 or 10 years old. In the beginning it was sad for us, but then I was happy because I could run. He did not like for me to run. I know it was because he wanted to protect me, but I liked to play and run a lot. Because Abuelita filled his place, I used to honor Abuelita, but not him. I have loved him all my life, but I was not honoring him because I thought he did not need anything from me. One day I realized I had to thank my father because he formed me. Then, when I became Christian, I knew the importance of honoring our fathers and mothers. So I started to honor him.

Love is honoring God the Father, Son, and Holy Spirit. Sometime after I started to read the Bible, Isaiah 29:13 was a frequent verse that God showed me. God says there that people love Him with their mouth and lips but not with their mind, heart, and soul. I used to say to Him: **"I love you God, so it is not for me."** However, of course He was talking to me. I was loving God in the wrong way. I was not loving Him with all my heart, mind, and soul. Even though I used to talk with Him about myself, I was not following His Word. As He said, "My people are destroyed for lack of knowledge."

When I knew Isaiah 53, I really felt I was living ungratefully with God and more with Jesus Christ. I felt a lot of pain in my heart understanding what Jesus did for us. He gave His life. He suffered for us. He was oppressed and He was afflicted, yet He did not open His mouth. He was brought as a lamb to the slaughter, and as a sheep before her shearers is dumb, so He opened not his mouth. It was painful for me because I was trying to defend myself every time someone wanted to hurt me or be unfair to me. So when I knew Isaiah 53, I said to myself: "Jesus did not open His mouth, even He was oppressed and afflicted. He gave His live on the cross for me, and I have been a badly grateful, unfair, and disloyal to Him. I have been believing and praying to imagens made by human beings when is

Jesus Christ who did all for me." Isaiah 53 showed me how to really honor Jesus and love Him with all my life. I am so grateful to Him for what He did for me and what He did for us.

CHAPTER 3

Faith and Obedience

"To have faith is to visualize, believe, and dream what you have envisioned within yourself. To have faith is to talk about your dreams with God because He knows more than you, and He wants the best for you. Faith is to walk in the paths that God has opened for you even though you do not know what you have to do. Faith is to continue walking and doing even though what you have to do is bigger than you. Faith requires you to act even though you are afraid, but you have to trust that God is with you. Faith is the only thing you have when it looks like you have nothing else. Faith is to believe in God but also to believe in you."

—Jackeline Alfonzo

Faith is action. The Scripture says that faith without works is dead. Also, it says that we have to walk by faith, not by sight. Faith in what? In what we hope for, *but* we must believe we will receive what we physically do not see yet. We must see with our spirit and our heart what God sowed in us. So you must feed it with the right seeds. Otherwise, circumstances or people around you will destroy it. If we do not couple our faith with our works, then we will not see what we believe.

For example, when I was a teenager, I dreamed of giving my mother and siblings a house and a better life. We did not have our own home; my parents were renting a house. Then after they got divorced, my mother, brother, and I moved to my grandmother's house (my mother's mother). However, for several familial reasons, we were moving from different houses. We did not have stability. Also, some days we had to live separated. My mother and siblings were with my aunt, my mother's twin, and I was with Abuelita. Then, in time, we were all together in Abuelita's house. Because of that instability, I started my communication with God. I was growing dependent on Him because I knew my mother was suffering for us. I wanted to protect her and my siblings. Then I started to talk with God a lot, asking and telling Him I wanted to study to buy a house for my mother and siblings, and I wanted to give all the best for them. As a result, I had the opportunity to study for the challenging career of petroleum engineer. It was not in my plan because I wanted to be a teacher. However, it gave me the opportunity to honor not just my mother and siblings but also my grandmothers, aunts, father, and everybody I could help. I did not know that because I was honoring my parents, God was blessing me with His promise. So since early in my life, He started to multiply the blessings He had been giving me.

> *But not everyone welcomes the Good News, for Isaiah the prophet said, "Lord, who has believed our message?" So faith comes from hearing. That is, hearing the Good News about Christ.*
>
> *—Romans 10:16-17 NLT*

We have to feed our faith with the seeds of God, which are His World and His presence. I can see it like a variogram chart, which is a tool I used during my professional career. To get a reliable variogram curve, a huge amount of oil/gas wells with valuable and abundant rock data are needed. Otherwise, the results of those charts are uncertain. In other words, the results of that reservoir study could have catastrophic final results. It is the same with our life. We ought to have our mind, heart, and spirit full of God and His Word. Then we can walk in His path and will, which are better than ours.

I will illustrate some examples of faith using examples of variograms curves. It is, the bigger the range, the better the correlation and the more reliable the results in technical terms. In terms of faith, it is equal to maximum actions of faith. Figure 1 is a real variogram to show it. The faith examples are from figures 2 through 5.

- A student who has finished his/her professional career has fed his/her mind with technical knowledge and maybe his/her spirit a little bit. So he/she would move to the next step of their life believing and trusting more in that technical knowledge. After that, the person stays in his/her comfort zone where it is calm and acceptable for them, but nothing more because they believe it is all they can get in their life. James 2:14 offers this consideration: What does it profit a man if he says he has faith, yet has not works?

Figure 2 shows this case. Each red point with the letter on the curve represents a step of belief or faith from that person. For example, analyzing the curve from the base to the top, the first point would be the person finished his/her study **(s)**. The next red point, the person got a job **(j)**. The next point, the person got his/her house **(h)**. The next point, the person got married **(m)**. Then, the last red point before the dotted lines of the chart, they had children **(ch)**. After the dotted vertical line, each red point represents the comfort zone of that person or family. The curve did not change. It is a flat line. This represents a relaxed zone for people. It is the comfort zone.

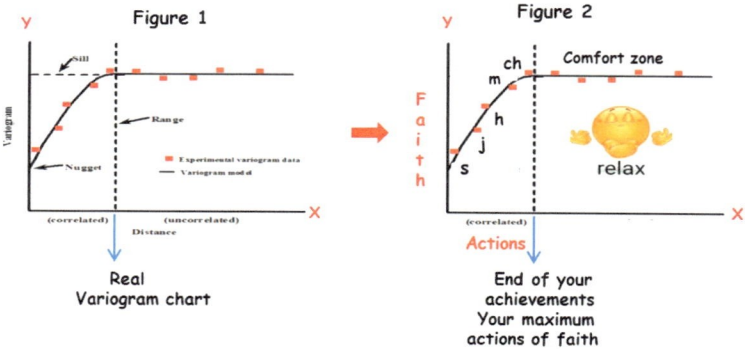

- The figure 3 represents another example of faith. Here, the person would achieve more **(X line)**. The faith is growing **(Y line)** until a maximum point **(magenta dot)**. This represents people who would have more achievements in their life because they have faith or reasons to take more action steps. However, for any unexpected situation in life, the faith curve after the maximum point starts to decrease. This represents that all their achievements were lost. The person at this step would have depression, sadness, fears, and no more faith. Also, that person might stop believing in God because he/she thinks God allowed them to lose everything. They might listen to what other people say to them about there being no more options for them to continue. As a result, those people never ever try again to achieve in their life. This happens because their faith was not strong enough. They did not feed their spirit with the Word of God.

Matthew 7:26 (KJV) talks about a foolish man who built his house on the sand and when the rain descended and the floods and winds came, they beat upon that house; the house was destroyed.

Another example would be the sandcastles built on the beach. That beautiful castle disappears as soon as a big wave comes ashore. This happens in our lives. Even when we have a lot of success during a certain period, if we do not feed our mind, heart, soul, and spirit with God's presence and His Word, then we will fall.

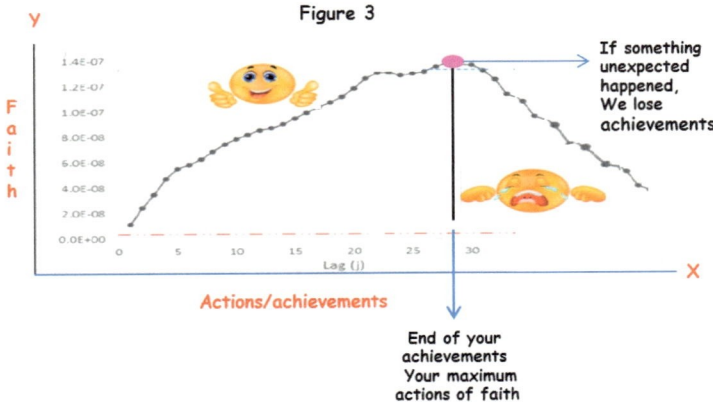

- Figure 4 represents the life of a person who has faith in himself/herself, and also in God, but he/she needs to consolidate it. Each face represents the same person but different season of his/her life, so even when that person falls, the only option for him/her is to rise again and continue. Proverbs 24:16 (NKJV) says: "For a righteous *man* may fall seven times and rise again." If that person does not strengthen his/her knowledge about God and relationship with him, then he/she will be living in his/her own forces without properly including in his/her life God Father, God Son (Jesus Christ), and God Spirit (Holy Spirit). When we do not know the root of why some hard things occur in our lives, and when we do not know what God tells us in His Word, we are working in our own strength. In this way, we live like we have learned from our parents, society, schools, friends, rest of the families, and the world. As a result, that person will not have the strength, wisdom, hope, and faith to continue despite the tribulations he/she faces.

The end of chart 4 shows at the base, a face with Jesus Rock announces, and the next face at the top, a face praying. This represents a transition state when people totally wake up from an inconsistent life with God to a deep relationship with Him where Jesus Christ and the Holy Spirit are included.

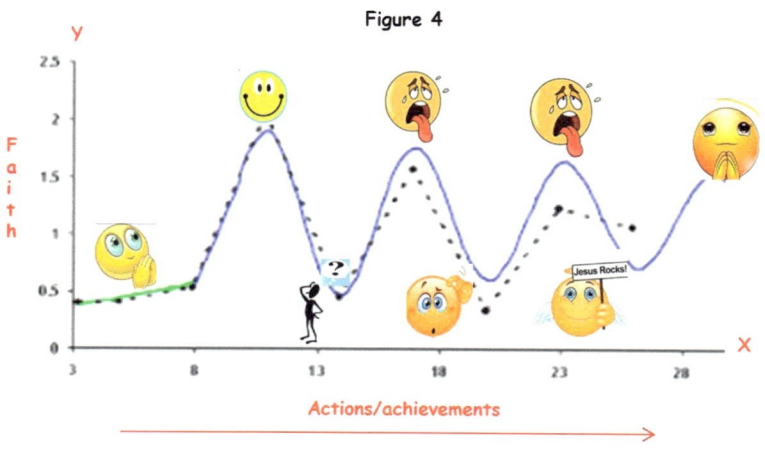

Figure 4

If you fall, you rise again, and continue

Chapter 3: Faith and Obedience

- In figure 5, people have a strong relationship with God. It is mandatory for them to have a consecrated life to God Father, Son, and Holy Spirit. Also, they include in their life the right people who help them to develop their faith and their strengths. Then, when a difficult situation or tribulation comes into their life, they still keep firm and strong because they rest in God's arms. They listen to the voice of God. They believe what Jesus said in John 16:33 (NKJV): "These things I have spoken to you, that in Me you may have peace. In the world, you will have tribulation, but be of good cheer; I have overcome the world." As a result, his/her actions are bigger. The blue curve growing on that chart shows a person's life flowing from glory to glory, as Haggai 2:9 talks about. Those people have edified their life on the rock of Jesus Christ. It is the faith that God wants us to develop. It is not easy to have God's joy while you see all the opposition to what God has told you; however, it forms part of your spiritual growth and relationship with Him. If we believe because we see, it is not faith. If you have joy just in good moments, but in tribulation that joy disappears, it is not joy. Our faith is tested by God, and it means that if we pass the test, we are going to the next spiritual level under His purpose.

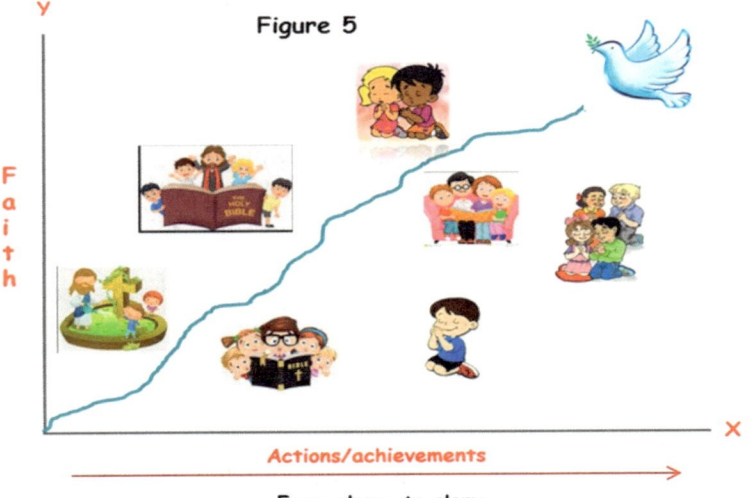

Figure 5

From glory, to glory

The more we seek God, the more our steps of faith grow. I grew up with a lot of faith. The tribulations of my life and my dependence on God built that strong faith. Also, in my opinion, dreams and faith are related because the more dreams you have, the more belief and actions you develop. First, I gave my mother a furnished house using my faith, communication, and obedience to God. In the middle of that, I helped my father to buy a used car. I did not have my own house and car, but my parents were my priority. Then I got my car totally new and better than I was expecting. One night I asked: "God, how am I going to have a house when my salary is not enough?" Then the next morning I got His answer. A co-worker by that time asked me if I had my house. I said not yet. She mentioned to me a builder who accepted a monthly payment plan. I could pay them the first part while apartments were being built, then I had to pay the bank the rest. So a new challenge of faith and obedience started for me.

In 2010 the economic situation in Venezuela was very difficult. Inflation started to increase without any control. Almost all Venezuelans were not happy with the president. Additionally, the control shift had started as well and the economic situation in Venezuela started to be more affected. By that time, I was working in Venezuela in a worldwide Oil Services Company where I moved in 2006. With my salary, I could cover the monthly payment for my apartment as well as take care of the daily needs of me and my family.

That year when the inflation was raised, I received my apartment. I was paying on the bank's home loan I had requested. Because of inflation, my salary was not enough to pay the bank, support my family, and pay the car insurance. I became desperate. But a few weeks after, I started to read the Bible. The more I read it, the more secure I felt. Every time the bank used to call me, I felt embarrassed and my answer was: "I am really sorry, but I do not have the money. I will pay as soon as I find the money to pay." Almost five months passed without a payment on the loan to the bank.

Trying to find a solution, I called some friends to ask for help. However, some of the answers were "no." Another answer was: "I have been interested in you for a long time, so we can try a relationship. I would like to marry you." I only found closed doors. The only open door was my Bible. The more I read it, the more I felt God was holding me by my hands.

Then I decided to quit my job. I wanted to go out Venezuela and study English to get an International job. The Latin America Geomarket manager would not allow me to leave, but she gave me the opportunity to be transferred. *Surprise!* I got a transfer to Egypt. I was extremely happy because I loved the Arabic music, the dance, and the food. So it was a dream come true. I said yes, but I talked with God. Then a few days before my travel, I asked God again if I should go to Egypt. He led me to Ezekiel 3:4-9 KJV: "And he said unto me, Son of man, go, get thee unto the house of Israel, and speak with my words unto them. For thou art not sent to a people of a strange speech and of a hard language, but to the house of Israel; not to many people of a strange speech and of a hard language, whose words thou cannot understand. Surely, had I sent thee to them, they would have hearkened unto thee. But the house of Israel will not hearken unto thee; for they will not hearken unto me: for all the house of Israel are impudent and hard-hearted. Behold, I have made thy face strong against their faces, and thy forehead strong against their foreheads. As an adamant harder than flint have I made thy forehead: do not fear them, neither be dismayed at their looks, though they be a rebellious house."

It was my first mature conversation with God where I understood that it was a commandment from Him. It was different from my previous conversation with Him because this time He was talking in a different way. In the previous conversations, He was just giving me what I needed without talking too much. However, I was happy after His answer. In my mind I remembered that where I was going, there was not hard language and that I would receive the crown.

Was it all beautiful during my time in Egypt? No, it was a challenge for me. It was not easy for me to work in Egypt because of how the manager was offering an Integrated Study to the client, which was technically impossible. The job there was harder than I expected. God let me know it with His answer when I asked Him. However, it strengthened my faith and obedience to Him.

I prayed to Him more. That difficult moment taught me that my co-workers and I were in the same hard situation. We all were suffering from that extremely inefficient way of working. We depended on one another, but at the same time, we just wanted to accomplish our tasks because we had to deliver. Some of them did not believe what I was telling them about the study plan being wrong. However, I started to feel compassion for my colleagues, and they also felt compassion for me. We, all of us in the study team, were working in a room. We started to help one another more. This was how I learned in Venezuela, but in Egypt, there was a new environment and manner of working. Additionally, I was the only woman on that team. Each meeting with the client was a battlefield for me and, I guess, for the rest of the team. We had to present to them our progress and results in their offices.

The meeting room had a long table. Each meeting was attended by 20 or more professionals from the client and those of us who were doing the study. Engineers, geologists, petrophysicists, supervisors, and managers were there. I was the only woman, a geomodeller and foreign in that team. Everybody talked in Arabic and at the same time. Each one of them gave their opinion. However, I could feel when they were angry and complaining about the project. The client wanted impossible results from what they had provided us with to do that study, and from our side—my supervisor and the rest of the team—we tried to defend our project. I knew they were talking about my area when they mentioned the word geomodeller and everybody looked at me. Otherwise, I was unable to understand anything. Of course, they talked and argued in Arabic. Suddenly, in our next meeting was one more manager from the client. He was from England. He was the manager of the client's entire team, so now everybody had to speak in English. Additionally, he was totally in agreement that the project had huge errors in terms of planning. He even said that it was crazy for a project of that magnitude to be done in two months when it needed at least one year. It was great for me because someone else agreed with my opinion. That person gave me the opportunity to explain my case.

One morning, before my co-workers and I went to the client offices, I asked my supervisor how to pronounce the word "uncertainty." I needed to talk about that in the meeting. So, my supervisor pronounced it for me before we went into the meeting. Then, as usual, the pitched battle started, but this time in English. I was sitting almost in the middle of that long table and my supervisor at the corner. I was able to understand more now what everybody was talking about. Everybody was discussing in loud voices. Then, in the middle of that discussion, I raised my hand to talk, but I had forgotten how to pronounce the word uncertainty, which was highly important to mention at that moment regarding the project. Everybody was in total silence. The British manager told them to listen to me, so they were waiting for what I had to say. I was immensely nervous. Of course! Each meeting made all of us feel nervous.

It was now my first opportunity to talk after several meetings, and I moved my chair a little bit so I could see the face of my supervisor and raised my voice to ask him, "Sam, could you please let me know how to pronounce the word I asked you about this morning?" Then... in that silent room where everybody was waiting for my project explanation, everyone started laughing at me. I'd taken a natural and genuine action. The amazing thing was that all the anger and discussion ended immediately because of what I did and said; it was so funny to them. This was not my plan, but in my weakness, I broke the discussion. For sure it was the plan of God. We are similar to the Apostle Paul, who had a thorn in his flesh that tormented and harassed him. He pleaded with God to take it from him; however, God answered him in 2 Corinthians 12:9 (AMP): "My grace is sufficient for you [My lovingkindness and My mercy are more than enough and always available regardless of the situation]; for [My] power is being perfected [and is complete and shows itself most effectively] in [your] weakness." Even in our weakness, the power of God is in our life.

With time, I understood God was strengthening my character, my relationship with Him, and my faith. I gained more technical experience about my job and gained a lot of life knowledge, too. My character was more mature than before. I showed them that my work was right even when they did not believe me, so the company received the extension to the next phase of the project from the client we were working for; and more projects from other clients. Also, after I received hard treatment from almost all who were my co-workers, God changed things for the better. I received from almost all of them their respect, their apologies, and their love. My heart was conquered by almost all of them.

Obedience and faith are highly related. For instance, when I made the decision to quit my job, it was because my faith was growing while I started to read the Bible. I believed God was holding my hand and that He was protecting me. Even though I grew up with faith, I needed another level of faith to make that decision. My family was depending on me, so to quit was risky. I did it because reading the Bible was my food. As a result of that leap of faith, I was sent to Egypt. The year before, I wanted to go there with my friends to a belly dance congress, but I could not travel because I did not have the money. However, God opened the opportunity to work there with an international salary. It was more than I was asking the previous year when my friends were traveling. Then one month after I started my job there, I could pay all the debt to the bank. I remembered some months ago when I was asking friends for help, but I did not receive it. The obedience, faith, and love were connected, and it was a blessing.

My main point here is not to talk about faith to get lots of achievements or to be successful in life, because a lot of information about that exists. There are people who have faith just in themselves, their capacities, and abilities. Other people have faith in idols or in talismans, or false gods and doctrines, and they are still really economically successful. However, it is a temporary state. The faith God is demanding of us to really be prosperous and stay on His path is to obey His Words and to believe what is written there. God asks us to believe in Jesus Christ and the Holy Spirit. Otherwise, we are building our house—life, city, country, and the world—on sand. God is asking us to build our life on the Rock, Jesus Christ, His Son. Similar to my example of faith where I mentioned the variograms chart, God left us plenty of valuable information in His Word. We must include this in our lives to avoid a catastrophic end that might also be extended to the entire world.

God is not looking for perfect people because He is the only perfection. He wants us to be brave and hardworking. He wants us to be willing to be guided, taught, trained, molded, cleansed, purified, disciplined, and loved by Him. He just wants us humble and obedient to Him. He wants people to spend time with Him. He wants people depending on Him. He wants people loving Him. He wants people having faith in Him. He wants people saying to Him, I did wrong, but I want to change, and I need you, Lord. The rest is His work. For Him, all is possible. We just have to believe in Him, but also believe in ourselves.

CHAPTER 4

Wisdom and Identity

"The fear of the Lord is true wisdom; to forsake evil is real understanding."

—Job: 28:28 (NLT)

The definition of wisdom is, the quality or state of being wise; knowledge of what is true or right coupled with just judgment as to action; sagacity, discernment, or insight. However, that wisdom would become earthly, natural (unspiritual), even demonic if we were not in God's presence. James 3:14 (NLV) states that if we have jealousy in our heart and fight to have many things, we must not be proud of it. But in the world, this is the wisdom that exists. We can find brilliant, dazzling, exceptional, famous, intense, and outstanding people, but without honor to God. This eminent wisdom is destruction for ourselves, the people around us, and the world. God is not expecting that we pursue that wisdom. He has for us the real wisdom. It is called the wisdom that comes from God. The fruit of this wisdom is people with purity, kindness, obedience, mercy, and peace. It's easy for us to conclude which one should prevail in us, in our family members, in our society, and in the world when we see the fruits that come forth from it.

God deeply loves His creation, and from the beginning, He showed it. For example, in the time of Adam and Eve, the earth was in disorder. It had corruption and violence. Only Noah and his family were living to venerate God. The rest of the people rebelled against The Lord's commandments, and a lot of sin existed. Then, God told Noah to build an ark. Genesis 6:14,17,18 (NLT) says: "Build a large boat from cypress wood and waterproof it with tar, inside and out. Look! I am about to cover the earth with a flood that will destroy every living thing that breathes. Everything on earth will die. But I will confirm my covenant with you." Then when the time had arrived, Noah, his family, and the animals entered to the ark. It rained forty days and forty nights. Then all was destroyed. However, those who were in the ark were safe. After one hundred and fifty days, Noah and his family came out of the ark.

God's purpose at the moment of creating the Earth and the humans was that we must be with His same character and behavior. The behaviour God is expecting from us is to live in mercy, peace, respect, honesty, and obedience. He is not expecting people to think they can do all they want and change the world as they would like with human rules. We must respect the rules from God. His Word is the same yesterday, today, and tomorrow. Humans must not try to change the world according to his/her natural wisdom. God avoided this in the past, and He will do it again if it is needed. He is not expecting that we show our capacity to transform the world, our life, our family, even our gender in a different way than what He said. He wants us to obey His commandments. People are doing and changing things according to their convenience, and they are avoiding God's commandments. However, similar to The Tower of Babel, God will show His power, and He will destroy all that is different from what He has established.

Noah and his family started a new generation of people after the deluge finished. However, again, people were doing wrong things. All of them talked the same language, and they agreed among them to build the Tower of Babel. They said in Genesis 11: 4 (NLT), "Come, let's build a great city for ourselves with a tower that reaches into the sky. This will make us famous and keep us from being scattered all over the world." However, the Lord God destroyed it because they disobeyed Him. He asked them to repopulate the earth instead of building that tower. God knew all their intentions of being like Him. It clearly showed that the ambition of some people had existed since the beginning of creation. They might think God is not watching us. However, Psalm 121:4 says: "Indeed, He who watches over Israel never slumbers or sleeps. He is always watching, and He takes care of us, His children."

Before Jesus Christ came, God chose a specific and obedient person to talk with him/her. Then that person talked with the rest of the people to relay what God was asking. For example, Moses, Esther, the prophets, and so on. After Christ was sent, we received the immense grace and favor of talking directly with God. However, we have to really believe in Jesus and the Holy Spirit of God. Jesus teaches us His wisdom that comes from God because He is the Word of God. Also, the more we are in God's presence, the more we will know God's plans, and we receive discernment and revelation from Him and His Word. The more we are in God's presence, the less arrogance, pretension, pride, ignorance, indifference, and wisdom in our own opinion exists. We must maintain our secret place to stay at Jesus Christ's feet. I have mine; it is my favorite place.

One day I heard that the dogs had a favorite place to stay at home. So, I can compare this with my case. At home, I used all spaces available to spend time with God, but I realized that I always came back to the place where I was closer to Him. When I think about it, when I am there, it is like if I can smell and feel Him there. It is an atmosphere from God created there. It does not mean that it is the only place I can talk with Him, but it is our place. It might be the same for each person who has his/her secret place with the Lord.

I would say there are two main groups of people in life. The first one spends time listening to Jesus Christ and learning about Him. The second group represents the distraction. What do you think God is saying with the quarantine? He is showing that we must spend more time with Him and less time in the vanities of life. We have been confined a little more than three months. This is a time when we should create the discipline to spend time with the Lord. It is an opportunity to create our secret places with Him and each day to go into His presence until it becomes a habit. This unexpected situation might open the eyes of all of us to reflect on how we have been living. It might open our eyes to see whether we are honoring God with our time. If we are not doing it, we must include it in our life as a priority. We must look for the wisdom of God and listen to our teacher, Jesus

Christ. We must start to live a balanced life where God is first, but we also have time for us, our families, friends, and people who might need help from us.

Luke 10:38-42 (NLT) discusses Jesus visiting His friends Martha and Mary. Mary sat at the Lord's feet while Martha was distracted by the amazing dinner she was preparing. Martha came to Jesus Christ and mentioned that her sister Mary was sitting with Him without helping her. Then, Jesus told her, "My dear Martha, you are worried and upset over all these details! There is only one thing worth being concerned about. Mary has discovered it, and it will not be taken away from her." Mary wanted to spend her time with Jesus listening to Him. What does this teach us? It teaches that we have to give our best to God as Martha was doing, but the most important thing is that we ought to spend time with Him to get His instructions to live a victorious and peaceful life. We find it at His feet, in our secret place with Him. Then in that place, He starts to comfort, cleanse, correct, edify, instruct, prepare, and strengthen us to be the best representations of God here on Earth.

> *"Woe to those who call evil good, and good evil; Who put darkness for light, and light for darkness; Who put bitter for sweet, and sweet for bitter! Woe to those who are wise in their own eyes, and prudent in their own sight!"*
>
> *— Isaiah 5:20-21 NKJV*

When I was at the university, I had to take a mandatory class to begin my petroleum engineering career. I heard from a professor on that subject. He was famous because all the students talked about him. However, no good comments were said about him. Even some students conducted protests against him. They said he was a very bad and unpleasant professor who did not want students to pass his class. I took the class with him because he was the only one. In my mind, it was all I heard about him. As a result, I did not pass the class. However, that semester let me know the truth about him. I saw and knew him as the best professor I'd had by that time. He really wanted to give us his best knowledge and advice. He asked us if we wanted to attend his class to occupy a chair, or if we wanted to really learn in order to become excellent professionals in the oil industry. Then the next semester, my mind was renewed, and I followed all his suggestions about the subject. I became one of his best students. During my stay at the university, I did not tell him that I was highly grateful for all he had taught us during his class. However, when I was working, I encountered him at one area of the company. I told him how grateful I was to him. I told him that he was an amazing professor, and he had taught me a lot. He smiled kindly, and he appreciated what I said. Some years later, he passed away. I was sad, but I thanked God He allowed me to tell him how valuable he was for me.

I would compare the experience of my professor with Jesus Christ. For example in the past, the Pharisees (or religious) didn't believe in Him nor love Him. In the present, it still happens. There are a lot of people who have not believed nor love Him yet. All of them need to receive a personal encounter with Jesus Christ. The only way we really know Him is by listening to Him. Then we win our own experience and opinion about His immense love for us. When we go to our secret place to take classes with Him, we can understand all He wants to teach us. He wants to give us the wisdom to form part of the family of God. He wants to return to us our real identity.

> ***"Let us honor and thank the God and Father of our Lord Jesus Christ. He has already given us a taste of what heaven is like. Even before the world was made, God chose us for Himself because of His love. He planned that we should be holy and without blame as He sees us. God already planned to have us as His own children. This was done by Jesus Christ. In His plan God wanted this done."***
>
> ***—Ephesians 1:3-5 (NLV)***

Identity is who we really are, not what society or people would say we are. Genesis 1:27 says that God created us in His own image. However, if people are disconnected from the source of God, they lose their real origin or identity. It is important to really know who we are. For example, a long time ago, I used to see people without a clear orientation, like a kite without the proper tail. It moves without a stable direction. I could detect when a person came to me without clear focus. Then, with my time reading the Bible, I knew about James 1:6 that says, who doubts is like sea waves blown by the wind from one part to another. I compare this to people without identity. They are easily dragged around by others. They might be living the dream of other people and not their own, which must be aligned with God's plan for them. Also, people who do not know their identity do not know their real potential nor the purpose God has for them. It is because they do not spend time in the presence of our Heavenly Father, God. At the end of this chapter, I show two figures that illustrate how some people are losing their identity because they believe and do what the system of the world says instead of what God says. However, it is not the only way of losing the identity left to us by God. Being slaves to sin means that people do not have the identity given to us by Jesus Christ and the Holy Spirit.

For example, in the book *Spirit of Leadership*, Dr. Myles Munroe talks about a lion that was lost when he was a cub. He was adopted by a sheep family. In time he became like a sheep. He was losing his real identity and his potential. However, one day his father, the lion, found him. Then he recovered his real identity because he was spending time with his real source and father. He knew he was a lion instead of a sheep. This is what Jesus does with us. He teaches us who we are and what we can do in Him. To know it, we need an encounter with Him. All of us need an encounter with Jesus Christ and the Holy Spirit, and when we ask God to show us the true, He gives us that moment.

The same year I was transferred to Egypt, the revolution started. After 30 years with the same president, the population started to protest against him. Cairo, the city where I was living, was in chaos. Because it was not safe for foreign workers, the company sent us to our original countries until the political and social situation got better. As soon as I arrived in Venezuela, I was assigned to a new project there. Then some months after, the company in Egypt got a project. I finished a project in Venezuela then traveled to Egypt, and vice versa. I was working for two countries, and even in the moment of that transition, I had to work with a project for Venezuela and Egypt at the same time because it was requested by the manager from Egypt. It was technically impossible, but God always helped me, and I could do it. If we ask God to help us, He does. Suddenly, my area of the project in Venezuela was stopped by the client for weeks because the input data

I needed to continue the project had to be redone. Then, I could focus on the project from Egypt. By the time I finished the Egypt project, the input data I needed to continue the Venezuelan project was ready. After that, the projects in Egypt were reduced because of the political situation; the foreign workers assigned there had to be transferred to another country. During that exhausting situation of working, God put in my heart to go to work in Africa. I had restricted my mobility to that continent because I was told by a person at the company that the place was dangerous. It was the continent where no employees wanted to go, but when we listen to the voice of God, we receive a paradise or gifts that others do not understand. I was immensely happy. I felt peace and joy in my heart. Some of my friends used to call me crazy for that. However, I was happy. I informed the career manager that I wanted to go there. Then, almost two weeks after, I got her email that an opportunity to be transferred to Angola had opened. They needed a geomodeler there. It was an amazing experience for me, but it was also my last station as an oil industry employee. After a deep and crucial conversation with God about I wanted to know more Him and the true of life, a few years after, I quit my job. I will give more details in chapters ahead.

After I quit my job in Angola, I kept working until I finished the project. That week when I sent my resignation letter, started my new level of communication with God mentioned at the Introduction of this book. For almost two weeks, I ate fruits, coffee, chicken, bread, and water. It was what my body was asking for. One night I entered my bedroom and felt something different there. I clearly remember when I was at the door of the bedroom. There was a light inside, and I said amazed. *"Jesús es un Rey y es el Hijo de Dios y yo soy una reina" (Jesus is a King, and He is God's Son, and I am a queen).* I did not know that He was the King. Even though I grew up knowing that Jesus was God's Son, this was like a revelation to me about Him. It was like I did not know it before. The surprising thing was that when I arrived in Venezuela almost two months after, my best friend invited me to church and gave me an invitation to an encounter there. It confirmed what I'd lived in my own encounter before. But in addition, I had my encounter with the Holy Spirit. I did not know Him. I used to hear the Holy Spirit's word, but I did not know who He was. The first time I knew Him, it was a totally amazing and unforgettable moment. Since that moment, I have known Him more and more every day. I say that my relationship with Him is from glory to glory.

Some people might say they know God. However, we must know God completely. Otherwise, we are without the identity He gave us. For example, I knew God, but inside me something more was missing. That part missing was my encounter with Jesus Christ and the Holy Spirit. The same happened to my dear aunt Dai.

My aunt Dai really did not know Jesus Christ and the Holy Spirit. As a result, she did not know her real identity. Also, she did not know God as Father. In her last months of life, when I was taking care of her, I gave her the gift of the encounter at the church. She went with her heart open to receive all in that event. She had her encounter with Jesus, and she met the Holy Spirit. This was evident to some people there. It made some of us cry tears of happiness. It was a victory for the Kingdom of God and for her. We saw when she received the Holy Spirit. It was amazing, with the signals from God. She was assigned almost the same chair and in the same line I was assigned to when I attended the encounter two years before her. The Holy Spirit strongly touched her. She experienced the same as me when He touched me. She could not control the movement of her legs. Then after that moment, I noticed she changed her way of praying to God each time she felt that intense pain of cancer. She was not praying anymore to a distant God. She discovered she was daughter of Him, so she cried out to God, calling Him Father. Romans 8:15-16 says the Holy Spirit tells our spirits that we are children of God. When I heard my aunt crying out Father, I knew the Holy Spirit had given her the identity of children of God. If you still do not know God as your heavenly Father, you have not received Jesus Christ nor the Holy Spirit. You must start a real relationship with God to get it. However, the velocity and cruelty of how human wisdom manages the world is against that.

Confinement has slowed the velocity of how people are living. It is like when I was working in Egypt, and then I went to Angola. In Egypt, the job was to hurry without rest, without time for anything more than surviving the job. Then I went to Angola, where a few weeks after I had arrived, I noticed a huge difference. It was a slow life rhythm for me. It was great. I found different challenges there, but I started to have a little more time to myself. The velocity of the life I had decreased there, allowing me to breathe easier and to talk more with God.

God allows things to happen because He wants to alert and protect us. Also, He wants us to seek Him. Maybe for Noah and his family, it was not comfortable to spend forty days and nights inside an ark with all kinds of animals during the deluge. Then they waited inside the ark one hundred and fifty more days waiting for the water to decrease. The noise and the smell of the animals, the sounds of thunder, and the movements of the ark on the water that they were living on for the first time might not have been easy for them. It was not comfortable for them, but it was needed for them to be saved. During that deluge, they had more time to pray to God, which allowed them to keep their hope and confidence in Him. In the present, I see people nervous and scared about the virus Covid-19, but we must know that when we are far away from God, the fear and lies easily enter us. The wrong seeds are sown. Then more and more seeds of sin grow up. I might call it virus or pests. We must worry about avoiding that kind of virus and pests. I would say that God is showing us the propagation of sin on the earth, but people without discernment nor wisdom of God cannot understand it. What happens outside is due to a reflection of each one of us inside. Pest is equal to sin. They are silent, but they are inside everyone who allows them to grow up in their heart, mind, soul, and spirit. If we are not in the presence of God, if we are not praying, if we are not renewing our mind with the Word of God, then we allow those tiny and silent germs to grow up until they become dangerous swarms inside us that would destroy us, others, and even the world. However, some people do not know about the real risk we have when we are not connected with our Abba Father, and we are doing what we want to do instead of what God asks us.

> *"My child, never forget the things I have taught you. Store my commands in your heart. If you do this, you will live many years, and your life will be satisfying. Never let loyalty and kindness leave you! Tie them around your neck as a reminder. Write them deep within your heart."*
>
> *—Proverbs 3: 1-3 (NLT)*

God is not expecting us to show Him our capacity for doing things or our human wisdom. He wants us to obey His commandments. He perfectly knows what we are able to achieve if we focus on something.

Proof of this includes when people wanted to build the Tower of Babel. They did not have the advanced technology that exists today; however, they were doing it with what they had. They had their human wisdom. They did not obey God. They did not want to depend on Him. Their arrogance of wanting to be like God or more than God was their guide. However, God Father, Jesus Christ, and the Holy Spirit confounded their language to avoid those people understood one another's speech. It was a division. That division shows the importance of the common language God wants all of us to have. It comes when our spirit is aligned with The Holy Spirit. Then, even though we would speak a different language, we easily communicate with the language of God. It is *love's language* that people and the whole world needs. It comes from Jesus Christ, and the Holy Spirit. It is what gives people the identity and fruit of God.

After forty days in the ark, Noah sent a raven and a dove outside the ark to see if the land was ready for them to go out. The raven and the dove were going and coming back to the ark because they could not find dry places. Some days later, the raven did not come back anymore to the ark, but the dove came back with a fresh green olive leaf in its beak. The raven is considered an astute and smart bird but not loyal. This is easy to see also with the history of Noah. The raven did not come back to inform them of anything. However, the dove came back with the olive that represented peace. The dove represents the Holy Spirit. Each one of us decides how we would like to live. We decide if we live like an astute and smart raven with human wisdom, or we decide to live like the dove full of peace, full of the Holy Spirit, with the wisdom of God. Our decision today will be the result of tomorrow. We must consider our life today but also the tomorrow of new generations as well. We must stop acting in selfishness without thinking about future generations. In that future generation are your children, the children of your children, and the children of their children, up to a thousand generations.

> *"Therefore know that the Lord your God, He is God, the faithful God who keeps covenant and mercy for a thousand generations with those who love Him and keep His commandments."*
>
> —Deuteronomy 7:9 NKJV

Chapter 4: Wisdom and Identity

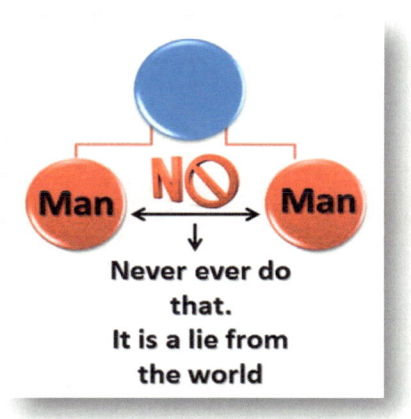

Man ⟷ NO ⟷ Man

Never ever do that.
It is a lie from the world

The Truth

God created human beings <u>in His own image</u>. In the image of God He created them; <u>male and female</u> He created them.

Then <u>The Lord God</u> made woman from the bone which He had taken from the man. <u>And He brought her to the man</u> The man said, "This is now bone of my bones, and flesh my flesh. She will be called Woman because she was taken out of Man." For this reason a man will leave his father and his mother, and will <u>be joined to his wife.</u>

Genesis 1:27 (NLT)
2:22,23,24 (NLV)

Woman ← NO → Woman

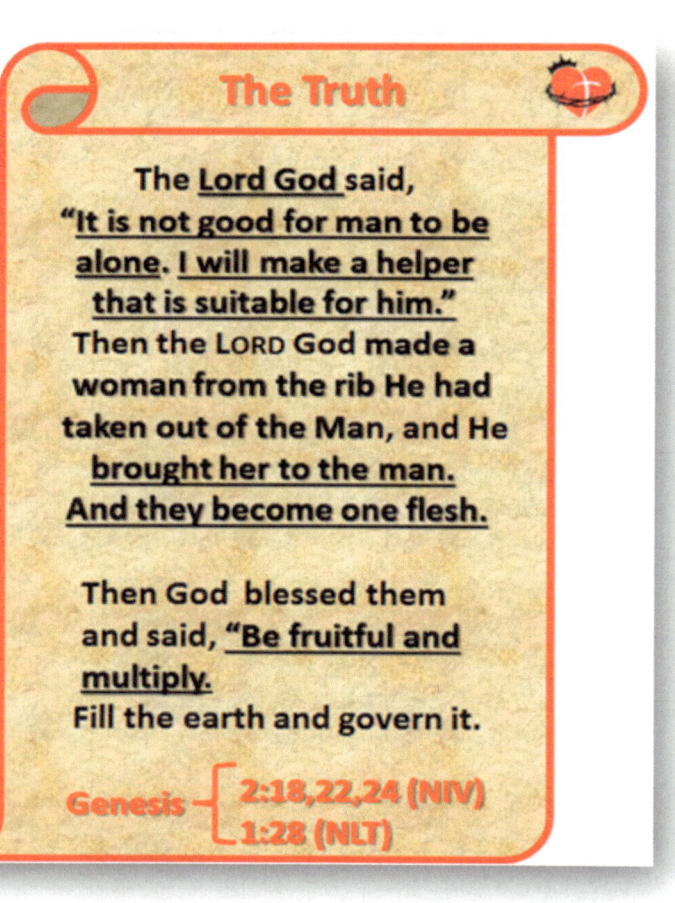

Never ever do that.
It is a lie of the world

The Truth

The <u>Lord God</u> said, <u>"It is not good for man to be alone. I will make a helper that is suitable for him."</u>
Then the Lord God made a woman from the rib He had taken out of the Man, and He <u>brought her to the man. And they become one flesh.</u>

Then God blessed them and said, <u>"Be fruitful and multiply.</u>
Fill the earth and govern it.

Genesis 2:18,22,24 (NIV)
1:28 (NLT)

CHAPTER 5

Death

"For the wages of sin is death, but the free gift of God [that is, His remarkable, overwhelming gift of grace to believers] is eternal life in Christ Jesus our Lord."

—Romans 6:23 (AMP)

In the beginning, God created the Earth: the day, the night, the sky, the earth, the trees, the sun, the moon, the stars, the animals, the man, the garden, and the woman. After God created the man Adam, He placed him in the garden. All the trees created by God were there. God also planted the tree of life and the tree of knowledge of good and evil. Then the Lord warned Adam in Genesis 2:16-17 (NLT): "You may freely eat the fruit of every tree in the garden except the tree of the knowledge of good and evil. If you eat its fruit, you are sure to die." After that, God created the woman Eve because God said it was not good that man was alone. Despite God's warning to Adan, Eve ate from that tree when the serpent persuaded her, and she also gave from that fruit to Adam. As a result, the sin of disobedience to what God commanded entered the earth.

God was not talking about a body or natural death. The proof is that Adam and Eve continued living after they ate from that prohibited tree. God was talking to Adam about spiritual death. It is the death that we must avoid. It occurs when we are disconnected from our heavenly father God. It produces sin. God is purity, mercy, favor, grace, love, peace, reconciliation, forgiveness, and holiness. He is without stains. He is perfect. All that is opposite to Him and to what He says to us is sin. That sin has origin when we disobey God's commandments, and when people do not believe in Jesus Christ nor the Holy Spirit. Then, that transgression produces a barrier between God and us because it is opposite to love, faith, and obedience to Him. So where there is sin, spiritual death is the result.

Sin is invisible most of the time. It is invisible for people who do not know the good and the bad, but God shows it to His people who He has prepared to know and see it.

I have a testimony about that, when God started to train me for how He would show me things. I was visiting my mother that weekend, so the night before I traveled back to my apartment, I had a dream with two young men I did not know. In that dream, one of them was dying. Other people were helping to place him into a car urgently. I just remembered his hair color that was extravagant and unusual. The next day, I stopped to buy cassava before my travel. Then, while I was waiting outside my car for my sister, who was buying it, I saw the two young boys I'd dreamed of the night before. They passed in front of me, and I was frozen when I saw them. Their striking hair color caught my attention. It was the same color I saw in my dream.

They were two homosexual boys. I did not do anything because it was so fast, and the dream came to my mind in that moment. I understood God was telling me that they were dying. I knew I had to stop them and talk to them about sin and the need for Jesus Christ, but it all happened so fast. I just prayed for them after that.

The sin entered the Earth when the snake, who represents the devil, told Eve that she could eat from the tree God told Adam he must not eat from. Adam told this to Eve. However, Eve was seduced by the snake that lied to her, telling her next in Genesis 3:4-5 (NKJV): "You will not surely die. For God knows that in the day you eat of it your eyes will be opened and you will be like God, knowing good and evil." Eve ate that fruit, and she gave it to Adam. The snake represents sin. It represents the devil. Those are the wrong voices that lead people to the opposite path of what God told us in His Scripture. To avoid it, we ought to develop discernment and wisdom. However, without spending time with God and His Word, we do not know what is true and what is a lie. So death is the result.

In Exodus 31:14, God commanded that we shall keep the Sabbath. This means people should not do anything that day. It is holy. If we meditate more on what God was asking, Sabbath is spending time with Him. In my opinion, it is not about a specific day. We ought to spend time every day with Him. Then, little by little, we feed our spirit. When we do this, we become more spirit and less flesh. We do more the will of God and less our will. As a result, we receive holiness.

When we do not feed our spirit, we are feeding our flesh. This separates us from our Heavenly Father. We very much need His nutrition. His Word is that spiritual nutrition all of us need. We all need to hear His voice, His advice, and His consolation. Jesus Christ is our water and our bread, so we need Him in our heart, our life. We need the Holy Spirit, who is our comforter, our mentor, our friend. He is who leads us to our purpose and God's plan for us. Without discernment nor wisdom of God, we easily open doors to sin.

I clearly understand this from my own experience before my encounter with Jesus Christ. When there was too much work, anxiety, and worry, I was not taking enough time in the presence of God, and I was not correctly feeding my spirit even though my love for God was great. I was walking and breathing, but through ignorance of the truth of God, inside me, I was dying. I opened doors to false doctrines, toxic emotions, and feelings that destroy. Those are some of the tiny viruses of the sin that kills people. However, when we spend time in the presence of God, we hydrate our body and spirit with His peace, hope, love, faith, mercy, favor, and grace. We clean our body, mind, and heart with the blood of Jesus Christ. Then, we will know that we can rest in His arms because we depend on Him, and He is faithful.

> *"And if it seems evil to you to serve the Lord, choose for yourselves this day whom you will serve, whether the gods which your fathers served on the other side of the River, or the gods of the Amorites, in whose land you dwell; but as for me and my house, we will serve the Lord."*
>
> *—Joshua 24:15 (AMPC)*

In the book *Tuesdays with Morrie*, the author states that "Everyone knows they are going to die, but nobody believes it." *And yes, it is true.* Some people live as if they are never going to die. However, it will happen to all of us. But people must know that we must live to save our soul; otherwise, we certainly die as God told Adam. When we live for Christ doing all God has commanded, loving Him, our life, and others, then that fear about death disappears. Living like this, we do not have to regret. Then we can say: "*I did all God asked me to do. I lived as God told me to live.*" Also, when we know the promise of eternal life in Heaven with God and our family, then that fear disappears. But to get that promise, we have a job to do. First, we have to save our soul, believing in Jesus Christ and being born again. Then we ought to teach and share the truth of God to our families, friends, and others in order that we can be in the presence of God, all together. This is what I am doing with my family and with each person I can.

Today, still, the enemy offers people things that are not true, as he did with Eve. All rules opposites to what is written in the Word of God, produce lies and sin. It is important that people understand that a life with sin and disobedience to God is death, even when we see them walking, eating, breathing, dancing, talking. It is important that people wake up and start to know the heritage that God gave us in His Word, so they can destroy any temptation coming from the enemy.

Chapter 5: Death

> ***Jesus answered him, "I assure you** and **most solemnly say to you, unless a person is born again [reborn from above—spiritually transformed, renewed, sanctified], he cannot [ever] see** and **experience the kingdom of God."***
>
> —**John 3:3 (AMP)**

The empty life I was living one day made me think that this was not the life I dreamed. I would say I was a successful professional; however, something was missing in my life. To finally quit my job was not an easy decision for me, even though I'd talked with God a little more than one year before. I decided on it for many reasons. First, I realized I did not study to become a slave to the job. Second, I was receiving injustices at my job. Third, my hunger and thirst for God were growing. I wanted to know more about Him and the truth of life. I also realized I was losing my best days with my family. The amount of work was consuming my life. And finally, I wanted to come back to my country and do amazing things to help that blessed land.

The second time I presented my resignation letter, I was working in loved Angola. The African Geomarket managers did not allow me to go, similar to the first time I quit. Then they gave me one week off. I went to South Africa because it is near Angola. I had a travel allowance benefit from my job, so I could do that trip. I went to Cape Town. It was amazing. It was a paradise for me. It was my first time since I started my professional career that I was without a laptop for work, without projects, without worries. I just was enjoying my life visiting wonderful and amazing places and eating delicious food. It was just God and me. So that week, I reflected. I saw that the life I had was not the life I wanted. I was always carrying a backpack with the laptop on my back. I did not want that weight with me anymore. I had to carry that laptop everywhere as if it was a baby. It was destroying my life. The laptop was more valuable to the company than the employees.

That heavy laptop on my back was taking my smile and my peace from me. During the few vacations I was allowed to take, I was asked to do jobs from home. I realized that I was spending more time with a computer than with my family. Also, on several occasions, some co-workers told me it was my baby. It was like I was married to a laptop.

I had to take it everywhere in every moment. It was not the life I dreamed of. I was a slave to the job and the people. Then, during those blessed days of vacation, I told God I wanted to see if everything would change. If not, I would move to another company or come back to my country.

That week was when Nelson Mandela, the president who freed South Africa from racism, died. All places in the city were honoring him. That same week during those vacation days, God was also breaking chains inside me. That week, God started the freedom in me. He started to guide me to His authentic peace, which does not depend on material, money, job positions, or earthly things that we would have achieved. He was leading me to His authentic peace that comes from Him, His Son Jesus Christ, and His Holy Spirit.

After that wonderful week, I came back to Angola to prepare my bags to spend Christmas with my family in Venezuela. I had bought my flight tickets earlier that year. In January, I came back to Angola to continue with my job. It was a new year, and I had hope in my heart that things would improve in my job. However, it was not like I expected. Conversely, it was getting worse after one year. I was in love with my career. However, I had to quit because I was receiving the same false promises and injustices. Nothing was changing compared to my beginnings with the company. Because of so many injustices and false promises, I had lost respect for the company I was working for, but I had to keep respect for myself, the client, and mainly to God. I had to keep my word with God about what I told Him almost one year and a half before. And for sure, He was reminding me of what we had talked about before. In case I had forgotten, He did not. It was a commitment with Him, so I had to do it. That decision was killing me. I had immense pain in my heart. I felt like I was dying because I was leaving something tremendously important to me. I saw my dreams get broken.

Those days of transition, while I finished all my commitments with the company and prepared to move back to Venezuela, were hard for me. In addition, I was waiting for my passport, which some months before was in the work permit renewal process. For some reason, I started to feel nervous about the flight I had to take to come back to Venezuela. After I had flown so much for work, why was I starting to feel nervous? The wrong voices in my mind were trying to make me feel nervous about flying.

During those days, my spiritual senses were opened more. I would say that after we take our next step of obedience and faith in God, He gives us our next gifts or weapon to continue growing in Him. Immediately after I quit, my spiritual senses were more sensitive to the voice of God but also to the wrong voices. Not all that happens to us is coming from God. Not all people who come to us are sent by God. Not all that we hear comes from God. Because I had been praying to God, I wanted to know Him more, and I wanted to know why injustices and bad things happen, He was answering my prayer. When we pray to God, He answers. I was taking my next steps to be led by Jesus Christ to His truth.

So, one day I was reading an email from a client who was wishing me blessings. In that moment, my supervisor was standing next to me, I clearly heard an internal voice that told me, *"Te vas a morir" ("You are going to die.")* Then I started to cry right there at work. I was nervous, confused, and afraid. A Venezuelan friend who worked there and another co-worker took me to another room. I asked them for a rosary because I used to pray it. My friend gave me his own, and I did not want that. I knew he was doing it in a kind gesture, but it was old, and I immediately gave it back to him. I wanted mine that was new, so they retrieved it from my wallet. Also, they gave me water. Some minutes later, I was better.

After that day, I was feeling nervous about the flight to come back to my country. I was praying a lot, asking God to protect me and all my things because I continued feeling and seeing something wrong with my travel and my personal things. I had sent to my apartment in Venezuela some household utensils with a shipping company, and I took my clothes with me on my travel. I was told that I would have my passport that week for my travel. However, the day of my travel arrived and still I was waiting for it. From the human resources department of the company, I got the information that I would get my passport at the airport, and one of the employees would stay with me there to wait for it. We waited hours at the airport, and by the time my passport arrived there, the flight was closed. However, they talked with the airline representative and I was allowed to board the plane. I was told that my suitcases would be shipped the next day. The human resource employee told me that as representative of the company he would send me the bags. I trusted his word and the company. However, the result of that was that I had lost all my bags at Angola's airport. I arrived in Venezuela just with my purse and the few clothes I had in my handbag. But God is always taking care of us; a friend recovered two of my bags some weeks after an insistent search of the airport.

I was totally destroyed by all I'd faced. This was when my best friend invited me to the Christian church. *"Wow! This is what I want,"* I said my first day there. The presence of the Holy Spirit, the kind people, and the Word of God touching and talking to my heart was giving me a new breath. My tears of hurt were changing to tears of cleansing and healing. Then I started a committed life of fasting, praying, worshiping, and serving God. He started to be first in my heart and life. From that moment, my life started to be ordered by Him. I was dying to my will and flesh to do the will of God. I began my new life.

Being born again means that we are crucifying our flesh, as Jesus Christ did on the cross for us. 2 Corinthians 5: 17 (NLV) says, "For if a man belongs to Christ, he is a new person. The old life is gone. New life has begun." We need to kill our flesh, which is to kill our earthly man. It is to kill our "I" matar nuestro "Yo" (Kill our I, our flesh). We have to die to our earthly passions and start to live heavenly passions. It is to live what Our Father's Prayer says "Hágase Señor Tu voluntad aquí en la Tierra como en el Cielo" (Thy Kingdom come. Thy will be done on the earth as it is in Heaven.) It is to stop thinking or doing what we want, and to start thinking and doing what God wants. It is to stop living for us, and to start living for God.

To kill our desires and our flesh, we must fast, worship, pray, and read the Bible. We must spend time in the silence and calm with God Father, His Son Jesus Christ, and the Holy Spirit. The verse Galatians 5:16-17 (NLT) says: "Let the Holy Spirit guide your lives. Then you won't be doing what your sinful nature craves. Our sinful nature wants to do evil, which is just the opposite of what the Spirit wants. And the Spirit gives us desires that are the opposite of what the sinful nature desires. These two forces are constantly fighting each other, so you are not free to carry out your good intentions." The noise just feeds our spirit with fear and lies. It does not allow us to clearly listen and see what God is talking about and showing us.

We are purified in several ways. It might depend on the purpose of each person, but it kills our flesh. The purification cleanses us of the root of bitterness. It cleans those areas that need to be cleaned in our heart and in our spirit. Why? Because God wants us totally clean of impurities to highlight our true origin or essence. It is like gold purification. The gold must go into the fire in order to remove impurities, and then the real beauty of that metal is the result.

For example, my dear aunt Dai had faced the purification of her heart, spirit, and soul before she died. That cancer made her suffer a lot. She had a lot of pain. She could not eat enough because the cancer was invading the space of her stomach and her other soft organs. Also, her leg was taken by that cancer because of a characteristic of that aggressive illness. The last two weeks of her life, she could not sleep. She spent nights groaning, and she was trying to keep silent because I know she did not want to make me suffer. However, I could hear her from my bedroom when I woke up during the night. Psalm 24:3-4 say, "To be in the Holy place with God, we must have clean hands and a pure heart." This Psalm speaks a lot. The Bible reveals small details that we would not see about how deep God is talking there. God clearly tell us that He wants us pure. He wants us without spots or wrinkles. He wants us purified. It was how He started His creation. He wants us transparent and crystalline without spots. This does not mean that He is doing wrong things to us. He is deleting and cleaning everything that is not from Him. He is cleaning and purifying us to come back to our essence, which comes from Him. That cancer was not from God. He does not send illness. He turns what is painful to us into our good. That unbearable pain and suffering was causing my aunt to love and depend more on God. He was cleaning my lovely aunt because there are promises to be in the Holy place with Him. She was purified.

In my case, I have been dying to my flesh since 2015 when I started a real relationship with Him, but also, each loss I have had in my life forms part of it.

My grandmother (Mamá) passed away on October 31, 2006. I lived in Maracaibo, which is an important oil city in Venezuela. I was working there. That weekend I was traveling to Venezuela's capital to attend a training. I was just arriving in Caracas on my way to a hotel when I received a call from my brother to tell me that Mamá was at the hospital. It was October 29, which is my birthday. She'd had a stroke.

She was in a coma and had severe brain damage. I told the company, and they were looking for airline tickets. However, two days after when I was having dinner with the team, my brother called me to let me know that Mamá had died. I went to my bedroom to call my family, but no one answered the phone. I tried to call a friend who I used to talk to, but she did not answer, either.

I was desperate, sad, and crying. I was alone. All my calls were unsuccessful. It was just God and me. It was my first time losing a family member who was deeply important to me. I did not know what to do. I spent that night just crying and talking with God. Then I traveled the next day for her funeral. As I mentioned in the chapter on love, I used to wake up after she passed away dreaming of her. I was sad when I had those dreams because I did not tell her I loved her. It stopped when one night I was dreaming again about her, and I could see her face in a picture. Her face was full of wrinkles in that picture, as she was before she died. In that dream she was telling me, *"Quédate tranquila, yo estoy bien, no llores y quédate tranquila porque yo estoy bien"* (*be quiet, do not worry. I am fine. Do not cry because I am fine.*) While she was telling me that, her face in the picture was getting younger. The wrinkles were disappearing while she was talking to me through her picture. Her face was getting beautiful without any wrinkles. It was soft when she finished talking. Then I woke up and never had sad dreams about her again.

My dear aunt Dai passed away on December 16, 2017. It was two days after a conversation I had with God and then her. After she died, I was hurt, defeated, empty, and broken. I was confused about if I obeyed and lived for God, then why didn't He heal her? When I saw her in the coffin, it was like I was seeing my dear aunt when she was a teenager. I did not remember her face when she was a teenager; however, she looked like a teenager. Her face was younger. That suffering face she had during that sickness disappeared, and now she looked like a beautiful angel. Early in the morning, the day of her funeral, I asked God why she died. The Holy Spirit showed me Isaiah 57:1-2 (NLT): "Good people pass away; the godly often die before their time. But no one seems to care or wonder why. No one seems to understand that God is protecting them from the evil to come. For those who follow godly paths will rest in peace when they die." During all her life, I saw in her a warrior who fought to have a better life. She wanted a better life for her family, her friends, and her neighbors.

Chapter 5: Death

However, the enemy was making her fall down. The lies of the enemy little by little were killing her. But in the end, she found the truth. She was tired of too much worry, tired of too much hard life. She was a warrior crossing a desert without knowing God as father correctly, but then she knew Him. She was a warrior who was fighting as a soldier. She was doing it without knowing the Holy Spirit, but then she knew Him. She was a warrior who wanted peace. She was looking for it without Jesus Christ, but then she found Him. She was a warrior who ran the good race of faith for her breathing because I saw her fighting to stay alive until the last second of her life.

My grandmother Abuelita passed away on October 27, 2018. I had been in the U.S. two months. I came to the U.S.A. because I'd won the Green Card Lottery. In 2015, a few months after I arrived in Venezuela, I received a phone call from a Visa organization. They told me that I was selected to participate in that lottery for the period of 2017-2018, but I had to apply first. I was surprised because I was not interested in coming to the U.S.A. and neither had I done an application, so I thought it was false. However, because they were calling me a lot, I started to pray and asked for answers from God. He led me to start that process for a Visa, and I did. I did not receive another call from them until 2017. However, honestly, I did not want to continue with the process. I was enjoying my family, my apartment, and my friends. I was growing more in my relationship with God Father, Son, and the Holy Spirit. Additionally, I was growing rapidly in the church. I started to pray more about whether to continue with the Visa application. The answer from the Holy Spirit always was yes. So I continued with the next steps. In the middle of that, the cancer came back to my aunt, and I was taking care of her. When we were at the hospital after her second surgery, I told myself that I would not send the form I had to complete for the Visa application. I did not want to go. However, always God reminds us of what He wants. The next day I told myself this, some friends of my aunt were visiting her. They started to talk about the Green Card application. I understood God was talking to me, saying I had to continue the application. Then I told Him: *"Dios, yo no quiero irme, no quiero continuar con la aplicación, pero completaré todos los pasos que me faltan porque quiero estar lista en caso Tú me necesites allá"* (God, I do not want to leave, I do not want to continue the Visa application, but I will complete it because I want to be ready in case you need me there.) I knew what it means to stay far away from your family and your country. I knew that one of the biggest pains in my heart was living far away from my family again. I knew that one of the biggest pains was to leave them again. I knew one of my biggest pain was that I could not hug and kiss them whenever I wanted again. I knew that one of my biggest hurts was leaving my old loved Abuelita because I had planned to stay near her until the last day of her life. However, it is not about our will, it is about God's will.

My Visa was approved on January 02, 2018. The organization was surprised because I was in the first group of people selected. I was planning to come in 2019; however, God was telling me that I had to come before. How? When you have been talking with Him for a long time, you know His voice. When we depend upon Him, we become familiar with how He talks. So I came in August to start my English classes.

When Abuelita died, my best friend called me. It was early, and I was sleeping, so she told me, "Amiga la Abuelita se fue" ("Friend, the grandma left.") I was silent and confused. How could Abuelita leave without me seeing her again? I asked God to allow me to see her in December when I had plans to travel for Christmas. I told her to wait for me. I asked when I was telling her that I had to come to the U.S.A., *"Abuelita yo vengo en Diciembre oyo" y ella me dijo "si mija te esperamos con los brazos abiertos"* ("Abuelita, I will come back in December, oyo," *and she told me,* "Yes, mija, we will wait for you with our open arms.") I was thinking about her Christmas gift. I wanted to buy her a soft blanket because I knew she would like it. Why did she leave without me hugging and kissing her again? I knew she was old, but I was not expecting her to leave us yet; especially without me hugging her again. I hugged and kissed her every time I could, but I wanted to do it again. All those questions came to my mind, but I could not cry. I just wanted to stay strong to search for an airline ticket and prepare my bag for travel. A friend sent me a message to say, if I was not able to travel, it was fine. However, if I was not in the last moment with my beloved grandmother, my life would be incomplete. She was a treasure to me. Also, I had to be with my family (mother's family and father's family), because for all of us she was an example. She was a mother for my mother, she was a grandmother for my other sisters. I knew I had to spend more money for the ticket, but God had been providing for me always, so I did not let that stop me. Then I called a friend who took me to the airport that afternoon. After I checked in, and when I was walking to the door waiting for my flight, I could not stop crying.

Her funeral was on October 29, my birthday. I wanted to give her the best coffin I could, but it was not possible. It was a simple coffin because of the difficult situation in Venezuela; only simple coffins were made there. I asked God through worship and prayer what He wanted me to say during the final remarks at her memorial service. Fisher of men (Lord, You Have Come to The Lakeshore) came to my mind. I had a lot of time without hearing that worship. She used to sing it at the church and when she was cooking or relaxing. Then, when the family, neighbors, friends, and I were worshiping God, I clearly heard it in my spirit that because of each time I went to church with her when I was a child. Every time she was singing there and in her house, she had sowed in me the seed of love for God.

Then, in the middle of too much pain on that day of my birthday, God gave me the amazing gift of giving me my answer.

> ***The word which came to Jeremiah from the Lord: "Arise and go down to the potter's house, and there I will make you hear My words." Then I went down to the potter's house, and saw that he was working at the wheel. But the vessel that he was making from clay was spoiled by the potter's hand; so he made it over, reworking it and making it into another pot that seemed good to him.***
>
> *—Jeremiah 18:1-4 (AMP)*

The book *Tuesdays With Morrie* reads: "When you learn how to die, you learn how to live." Life has been teaching me to die in different ways, and even when each of those moments was killing me, I was growing in my relationship and dependence on God. To learn how to die is to tell God: "I am here dear Father. You are the owner of my life. I want to be the person you created, so give me strength to do your will instead of mine. I am in your hands."

When my friend kindly gave me his old rosary that day at the office, I could not keep it in my hands. I rejected it, and I gave it back to him immediately. I wanted mine that was newer. My friends gave mine but also a glass of water to calm me down. But that time, I did not know I was dying to my old life of being a religious person who used to pray hundreds of times the rosary but not loving or honoring God from my mind, heart, and soul. By that time, I did not know I was leaving a life based on broken cisterns that do not retain water to start a life full of living water that only God Father, God Son, and the Holy Spirit can give us. By that time, I did not know I was leaving my old life of the flesh to start a life of holiness to really please God. Today, millions of people walk, work, breathe, eat, write, read, and so on, but they are living disconnected from our source, God. They do not believe in Jesus Christ nor the Holy Spirit, so they are spiritually dead. If they really want to live, they have to die to their flesh and become a new person in Christ. When God sent His Son Jesus Christ to die for us on the cross, He was telling us how much He loves us. God is love, but He is a consumer of fire, too. What does this mean? It means that the sin activates that consuming fire of God. God wants us to live in holiness because He wants to protect us from His consuming fire. People are waiting for a vaccine to combat Covid-19; however, the only vaccine that we need is in our hearts. The only vaccine the world needs is a grateful heart to value what Jesus Christ did for us on the cross. The only vaccine the world needs is wisdom to know that Jesus redeemed us to God by His blood, and that blood has a high price.

> *"Blessed [anticipating God's presence, spiritually mature] are the pure in heart [those with integrity, moral courage, and godly character], for they will see God."*
>
> *—Matthew 5:8 (AMP)*

CHAPTER 6

Forgiveness

"Then Peter came to Him and said, 'Lord, how often shall my brother sin against me, and I forgive him? Up to seven times?' Jesus said to him, 'I do not say to you, up to seven times, but up to seventy times seven.'"

—Matthew 18: 21-22 (NKJV)

I grew up reciting the Lord's Prayer. When God opened my eyes that day in front of my work station, a lot of revelations came to me, including the meaning of that prayer. It contains all we need. However, it must not become a repetition without understanding the deeper meaning.

The disciples of Jesus Christ asked Him to teach them how to pray. Then Jesus led them to the Lord's Prayer. See figure 1.

> **The Lord's Prayer**
>
> Our Father in heaven,
> Hallowed be Your name.
> Your kingdom come.
> <u>Your will be done
> on earth as it is in heaven</u>.
>
> Give us day by day our daily
> bread. <u>And forgive us our sins,
> For we also forgive everyone
> who is indebted to us.</u> And
> do not lead us into temptation,
> but deliver us from the evil one.
>
> Luke 11: 2-4 (NKJV)

Figure 1. The Lord's Prayer

Then I said to myself: "How can we ask God to forgive us if we do not forgive others? Who are we to pretend God forgives us, but we are not able to forgive others?"

We ought to know that the devil, our real enemy, is always trying to destroy, and he knows the areas where we may be hurt. The devil uses all we have as first place in our hearts and the people who are nearest us to sow seeds of bitterness or unforgiveness. So when we deeply love God and we are humiliated and surrendered to Him, the enemy does not find open doors in us to enter. Even when he would try to enter, we have the weapons to fight against him. Those weapons are our identity in God. Those weapons are our faith, our hope, our prayer, our love. Those weapons are our time with The Lord. Those weapons are our fasts to seek the presence of God to sharpen our spiritual senses, so we can see what He sees and listen to what He says, and we can speak what He speaks. As a result, the enemy runs away from us. We close doors to the enemy when we show him that we know who we really are and what we can do in Jesus Christ.

For example, before I knew the importance of obeying the Word of God, I was not honoring my father as I had to do. Also, I did not talk with him a lot. I just had short conversations with him. But then, I understood that we are representing Jesus Christ on Earth, so we ought to show our changes to other people. Also, we ought to share the Word of God with everybody who allows it. I started to talk with my father as much as I could. One day, I was talking to him and realized that He was laughing. He was making fun of what I was saying to him. I continued talking, but he continued doing that. Then I noticed that it was not the way he was with us. He liked to talk with his children and listen respectfully. So I said to myself: *"Este no es papá" ("It is no dad.")* Then I immediately prayed in the name of Jesus that all that was not from my father go out of him. And it was surprising how papá was quiet and silent. His face and attitude changed. After that, he was as he is normally with me, and we continued the conversation in peace.

In books one and two of Kings, I noticed that some generations were offended and disobeyed God; however, always there was one King who totally ruled the nation according to God's commandments. In those books, we can easily see the degradation, distortion, and disorder in the nation when kings ruled disobedient to God. Then we see the change in order and restoration of the nation when a king who obeyed God was the ruler. I see it happen in families. Most of the time, there are some members that wake up to the truth of God, and they must wake up the rest of the family. So when I woke up, I started to wake up them. My dear aunt Dai was one of the first. She was allowing seeds of bitterness to be sowed in her mind and heart by the lies of the enemy. Those seeds were not giving life to her. Proverbs 4:23 says that from the heart flows the springs of life, so keep and guard it with all vigilance.

"Forgive yourself before you die. Then forgive others," it says in the book *Tuesdays with Morrie*. I would say this is similar to what the second commandment says: "Love others as you love yourself." In my opinion, when a person does not know how to love him/herself, that person does not know how to love others. Then they do not know the importance of forgiveness. They might not forgive others but also themselves. I did not know the importance of forgiving ourselves. I learned it at the church. I started to ask the Holy Spirit to show me the areas I had to forgive myself, and I did. I taught it to my beloved aunt, my mother, father, and uncles, too.

The enemy attacked my beloved aunt Dai strongly through her relationship with her brothers and even with Abuelita. The communication with her brothers was degraded. Then, this started to create discussions, confusions, and unforgiveness among them. I told her several times that she needed to forgive. She was suffering because, similar to me before, she did not understand why bad things were coming into her life. She did not know why communication was bad with her brothers when they loved each other. She did not know who the real enemy was. Before she became sick, I used to explain to her the importance of forgiveness and why inconveniences were happening with her and her siblings, but she kept thinking her brothers did not love her. They also thought Dai did not love them. Those wrong seeds were growing in her mind and her heart. The consequence of it was that aggressive cancer. But God always is merciful. He allowed her to stay with me those four months after her last surgery so she could attend the encounter, the services, the intercessor prayers, and the friendship group. She was renewing her mind, her heart, her spirit, and her soul with Jesus Christ and the Holy Spirit every day during that time. Those months that she was with me, God was cleaning her. Jesus Christ was working on her heart. And she knew Him as a Father and friend who really and deeply loved her.

One of my prayers to God is the restoration of my father and uncles because they are separated. Even when Dai and Abuelita passed away, they were divided. They all had forgotten their origin. They forgot how much they loved themselves. They forgot that they were born from a woman of love, who deeply loved each one of them. I know they deeply loved her, but the sin in them covered their hearts from seeing the love among them. They have allowed other people to interfere among them. They have allowed that voice from other people to divide them. They have allowed the voice of the enemy in their minds to lie to them, and they have pain among them. They have not realized yet that even though they did not grow up with their father, they have their Heavenly Father waiting for them. Psalm 27:10 (KJV): "When my father and my mother forsake me, then the Lord will take me up." So, if they are not in a deep relationship with God, they are not able to see and hear what they must hear from Him. However, I have faith and hope in God that their hearts will be for God. Then they will discover the love of God for them. I believe they will forgive themselves, and they will remember their love for one another.

Chapter 6: Forgiveness

In December 2019, I attended a presentation given by the Christian author, Devi Titus. It was about preparing the table for family. That morning when I was preparing my breakfast, I heard: *"Tú lo vas a arreglar" ("You are going to fix it.")* I did not know what God was referring. On my way to the church, I was praying and asking Him for clarity. Then at the presentation, it was clear when the Holy Spirit told me that I had to prepare the table for my father and uncles in my grandmother's house. I did this, obeying and believing in Him. I invited them for a Christmas dinner. Also, I invited my brother, my cousin, and one of my nieces. This was in faith because my previous meeting with my father and two uncles was not a good experience for any of us. However, I acted in faith and obedience to God. I bought here in the U.S.A. beautiful plastic red plates and some other things for the dinner. However, my father did not attend. He told me he had another commitment. It deeply hurt me, but I knew I had to keep strong. God had been teaching me to keep strong. So the dinner was done with the rest of my guests. At the moment of dinner, we went to the table. When we were sitting there, I had a really amazing sensation. It was beautiful. It was a simple table with food, and for the first time we were sitting together there at my grandmother's house. Then all of us were silent. I guess that like me, their minds were passing beautiful moments with Abuelita, Dai, and all of us together. Some minutes after, I started to pray. I was giving God thanks for all His blessings. I read Isaiah 53:3-7. I talked a little bit about forgiveness and what Jesus Christ did. Even when He was abused, betrayed, and beaten, He did not open His mouth. He did not say anything. He did not defend Himself. Then we started to eat. It was an amazing moment. I saw my uncles sharing food and filling their glasses with soda.

I have been helping them with a soul healing. I have been calling each one of them and talking to them about the love of God and what unforgiveness does. I pray with them. Also, I ask them to repeat that they love each other, and that they are loved by God. Sometimes the enemy has tried to make me stop believing, but I only believe what the Holy Spirit told me. God is working on them because I know how much they love one another. Because I am persistent in believing and praying, loving, and explaining Jesus Christ to them, I am able to learn and see with my spiritual and physical eyes what God has spoken to me.

When Abuelita and Dai were alive, we used to eat some days at the table, but most of the time we were at the back room of the house because it was the coolest area there. However, in my mother's house, the best place to gather has always been in the kitchen. We were always at the table while my mother or my sister was cooking. Even the kids of the family enjoyed the kitchen. We loved being all together, sharing with her and with one another. Laughing about our life experiences, the kid's actions, and joking. After we knew the truth of God, we included prayers and praises to The Lord because we must keep up our family protection fence. The enemy is like a roaring lion trying to destroy people and families, and we must fight with the weapons of God to avoid it.

> ***"For to us a Child shall be born, to us a Son shall be given; And the government shall be upon His shoulder, And His name shall be called Wonderful Counselor, Mighty God, Everlasting Father, Prince of Peace."***
>
> *—Isaiah 9:6 (AMP)*

In his book *Storm Warning,* Billy Graham talks about all the possible solutions that the world offers to people to be in a better soul healing condition. Good books, good physical condition, good psychological wellness, and so on might help people temporarily. Those are the solutions according to people who do not know Jesus Christ.

The real solution is written in the Bible. God sent His solution 2,000 years ago. However, people have their eyes closed. People need healing from the root. The healing that is needed in the world is in the heart, mind, and soul of the people. Millions of people ought to forgive. Millions of people believe that it is right to keep resentment against families, friends, governments, and even themselves. Unforgiveness is a huge sin, and some people do not know it.

This sin is filling the hearts of people. People have to repent. I see it like the fat in a body. Each one of us has muscle; however, when people eat a lot of bad food and bad fat, the muscle starts to disappear. When people do not eat healthy, they cannot see their beautiful muscles or the real shape of their bodies. It is similar with our heart, our mind, our spirit, and our soul. In the heart of a person, fat represents an unhealthy lifestyle, sickness, anxiety, and distance from God. If we don't feed it with the bread of life, Jesus Christ, which is the bread coming from heaven or good seeds, then the heart, mind, spirit, and soul will form layers of sin. That sin is equal to fat. Sin hides the true beauty of your heart, mind, and soul. Each one gives what they have. If unhealthy seeds or information is coming there, nothing healthy is going out.

Jesus Christ wants our heart, and we have to open it to Him and the Holy Spirit before it is too late. God says in Joel 2:12-13 (NLT): "Turn to me now while there is time. Give me your hearts. Come with fasting, weeping, and mourning. Don't tear your clothing in your grief, but tear your hearts instead. Return to the Lord your God, for He is merciful and compassionate, slow to get angry and filled with unfailing love. He is eager to relent and not punish." Our life is our personal and own project. We must stop and analyze how we are living. At this moment with COVID-19, God is talking. Also, He has been talking with the forest fire in the Amazon in 2019, in Australia 2019-2020, the locusts that crossed Africa 2020, with the political situations in different countries, and with the distortions about how some people are living. God speaks clearly. God said in Deuteronomy 30:19 NKJV: "I call heaven and earth as witnesses today against you, that I have set before you life and death, blessing and cursing; therefore choose life that both you and your descendants may live." However, when a person has his/her heart, mind, and soul full of vanity, unforgiveness, and another kind of sin, she/he cannot understand what God is talking about. God also said in 2 Chronicles 7: 13-14 (AMPC): "If I shut up heaven so no rain falls, or if I command locusts to devour the land, or if I send pestilence among My people, If My people, who are called by My name, shall humble themselves, pray, seek, crave, and require of necessity My face and turn from their wicked ways, then will I hear from heaven, forgive their sin, and heal their land." Are you doing it?

> *"And you He made alive, who were dead in trespasses and sins, in which you once walked according to the course of this world, according to the prince of the power of the air, the spirit who now works in the sons of disobedience, among whom also we all once conducted ourselves in the lusts of our flesh, fulfilling the desires of the flesh and of the mind, and were by nature children of wrath, just as the others."*
> —Ephesians 2:1-3 (NKJV)

Ephesians 2 talks about the prince of the power of the air, who works in the children of disobedience. The devil works and easily manipulates and uses people who disobey God's commandments. The devil is using a lot of people to bring about sin, to create disorder, to hurt others, and to control the whole earth. Did you know that the devil is real and he works with some people who do not believe in God? I did not know this. I did not know that when we disobey God's Word, we open doors to the devil. As a result, a lot of cruelty and disorder exists when those doors are opened. The devil and its demons act. I thought all that happened in the world and in us was done by God. When we really know the inheritance God left us written in His Word, then we learn the truth of life. He left us the blessings and the curses there. Matthew 24:35 KJV says: "Heaven and earth shall pass away, but my words shall not pass away." I also knew that the devil is always trying to hurt our hearts. His main purpose is to create unforgiveness there, and it destroys people.

When I was a kid, I had a dream where I was walking through a beautiful path like a bridge. It was very close to the water, and it was narrow and bright. In that dream, I knew I was walking to the sky. The floor of the bridge was shiny. Both sides were full of beautiful flowers, and the river was like a mirror. It was bright. At the end of that bridge was the devil. It was like people describe. That ugly image stopped me and told me it was not my turn yet. Then I woke up. I was wondering why, if I was walking to the sky, I was stopped and told that it was not my turn by the devil instead of God. However, when I became Christian, I knew that it was because the devil is considered the prince of the air. Since I was a child, I have been facing difficult situations, and several enemy attacks. I didn't know who was causing them. It was one of the reasons why I was interested in knowing more about the truth of life. I wondered why, when I was trying to have a quiet life, a lot of bad things were coming to me. Then God showed me that our real enemy is the devil. Jesus Christ says in John 10:10 (AMP): "The thief comes only in order to steal, kill, and destroy." The Apostle Paul advises in Ephesians 6 that we have to put the full armor of God that allows us stand to up against all strategies of the devil. The real enemy wants to destroy families, friendships, people, churches, and the world. That enemy was telling my aunt a lot of lies, even me. We all have to open our hearts to the truth to stop that. People have to come back to pray, fast, love, and forgive. People must start to fight against the real enemy that wants to destroy our peace. When I knew the truth, I stopped sinning and fighting in my strength, the flesh, and I started to strengthen my spirit to fight with the weapons God left us. Zechariah 4:6 KJV says: "Not by might, nor by power, but by my spirit, saith the Lord of hosts." It is time to fight on our knees, with the power of the Holy Spirit and the Word of God.

"Her sins, which are many, are forgiven, for she loved much; but he who is forgiven little, loves little," Jesus Christ says in Luke 7: 47 (NLT)

The scripture Luke 7:47 was what Jesus Christ did for me. Proverbs 14:1 (NLT) says: "A wise woman builds her home, but a foolish woman tears it down with her own hands." I was being a foolish woman because I did not know the heritage that God left us to be wise. I was not honoring Him as He asks. However, Jesus Christ rescued me. He forgave me. He washed me. He gave me back my identity, dreams, essence, and peace. It is why I love Him with my entire mind, heart, and soul. It is what He does for each person who opens his/her heart to Him. It was what He did for my aunt, and even when she passed away, she was alive. Jesus saved her. She decided to open her heart to Him, and then He started to clean it. Then she could see the love for her and the love for her brothers. She left the earth in peace because she decided to forgive.

The Lord's Prayer is a simple but deep test that allows us to see where we are with God. We must understand what Jesus Christ wanted to tell us with this prayer. When you pray it, are you doing what it says? Are you recognizing God as our Heavenly Father? Do you really know He is our Father? Are you honoring Him as Holy? Are you worshiping Him as Holy? Are you asking Him for His Kingdom? Do you desire His Kingdom in your life, your family, your home, church, your city, and your country? Are you showing God that you really want His Kingdom here on Earth? Are you really allowing God's will in your life, or are you doing your own will? Are you talking with God about all your needs? Are you resting in Him while you do your part for your needs and trusting that God does His part? Are you thinking about how you are acting with God, yourselves, your families, friends, neighbors, co-workers, sisters and brothers in Christ and others? Have you forgiven yourselves and others who would offend you? Have you thought about why you have to expect God to forgive you if you do not forgive others? Are you living far away from sins? Are you feeding your spirit in the presence of God? Are you spending time with God to avoid temptations and sins? The Lord's Prayer is not just to repeat ten or more times without the discernment and wisdom of that valuable, important, and revealing prayer. It is time to leave the religious life and to start our deeply honest, consecrated, loyal, grateful, and true relationship with God. It is time to leave our comfort zone about God in our life, houses, and churches, sitting on soft chairs, sofas, and beds while people who do not believe in God and people who say they are believers are creating false doctrines and are worshiping the devil on their knees. How can God forgive our earth if His people are not doing what we must do? How do we pretend to extend the Kingdom of God if we are in our comfort zone? How are we expecting every knee to bend before Jesus Christ if we, the army of God, are not doing it?

CHAPTER 7

Process

"O righteous Father, the world doesn't know you, but I do; and these disciples know you sent me. [26] I have revealed you to them, and I will continue to do so. Then your love for me will be in them, and I will be in them."

—John 17:25-26 (NLT)

We were created in the image of God; however, the wrong information coming from our choices, decisions, families, societies, religious leaders, nation's leaders, friends, and others have caused us to lose our origin, our essence, our purity, and our real identity. Each purposeful life must have a process. *Some words that define process are: Progress, advance, go forward, and go towards a certain end.* This means we have a beginning and an end point. First, we are chosen by God before we are formed in the belly of our mother. Jeremiah 1:5 (NKJV): "Before I formed you in the womb I knew you; before you were born *I sanctified you*; I ordained you a prophet to the nations." After we are born from our mother, our flesh birth, we must be born again from water and spirit. Jesus cleans our sins with His blood, but we *must* take an additional step: In John 3:5-6 (NKJV), Jesus said, "Most assuredly, I say to you, unless one is born of water and the spirit, he cannot enter the kingdom of God. That which is born of the flesh is flesh, and that which is born of the spirit is spirit." To be born again is to stop our desires and will to do the will of God. Most of the time, it hurts. It is what I mentioned in the chapter on death. It is needed to enter into the Kingdom of God.

Jesus is our best example to follow. He denied himself. He resigned His divine privileges as God, and He was born as a human being to save humanity. He was born from Mary, an obedient and wise woman, who obeyed the will of God instead of her own. Additionally, she showed that Jesus Christ is who we ought to obey. She said in John 2:5 NKJV: "Whatever He says to you, do it." She was telling us that we must do all that Jesus Christ says. It is the Will of God from the beginning of creation. In the Old Testament, God left us His ten commandments. **See figure 1**. Then when Jesus Christ came, He summarized it in two. He said in Mark 12:30-31 that we shalt love God with all our mind, heart, and soul. Also, we shalt love our neighbour as we love ourselves. It is easy to see that when we obey the two commandments Christ left directly, we are obeying the ten commandments God gave us at the beginning. The commandments are the starting points from God to measure where we are in Him. So, the more we honor our origin, the more wisdom, peace, and joy we have during our process. This is because we know God is walking with us during those moments.

The Ten Commandments

"I *am* the L<small>ORD</small> your God, who brought you out of the land of Egypt, out of the house of bondage.

1. "You shall have no other gods before Me.

2. "You shall not make for yourself a carved image any likeness of anything that is in heaven above, or that is in the earth beneath, or that is in the water under the earth. You shall not bow down to them nor serve them. For I, the Lord your God, am a jealous God, visiting the iniquity of the fathers upon the children to the third and fourth generations of those who hate Me, but showing mercy to thousands, to those who love Me and keep My Commandments.

Exodus 20:2-17 NKJV

The Ten Commandments

3. "You shall not take the name of the Lord your God in vain, for the Lord will not hold him guiltless who takes His name in vain.

4. "Remember the Sabbath day, to keep it holy.

5. "Honor your father and your mother, that your days may be long upon the land which the Lord your God is giving you.

6. "You shall not murder.

7. "You shall not commit adultery.

8. "You shall not steal.

9. "You shall not bear false witness against your neighbor.

10. "You shall not covet your neighbor's house; you shall not covet your neighbor's.

Exodus 20:2-17 NKJV

Figure 1. The Ten Commandments of God.

I see the laws and commandments of God as a perfectly straight line that allows us to know where or how we are with God. I am going to illustrate it with the figure 2. **Case 1** shows how the closer we are to the brown line, the closer and more obedient we are to God. **Case 2** shows a visual warning report allowed by God in 2020. With the social distancing and mask requirements established when Covid-19 started, God showed us how humanity is at the moment. He also showed us the solution. The confinement represents God asking the whole world to come back to Him, obey and spend time in His presence. Most of the people are not obeying the two commandments told by Jesus Christ. There is not real and sincere consecration and love for God. Therefore, people really do not know love themselves, so they do not know love for others. As a result, when we disobey God's commandments, a barrier, separation, and division exists between God and us. It is sin. The figure is like a thermometer to measure our temperature. So the laws and commandments of God are equal to a thermometer. It is the thermometer of God to people, families, societies, cities, and nations that allows Him and us to measure our obedience and love to Him. God measures the magnitude of sin in us and the earth.

What is God talking about? He is saying that sin is invading the earth, so process times will be more evident. The solution? People must spend more time at the feet of Christ; more time in the secret and silent place with God and less time in the noise of the world's system.

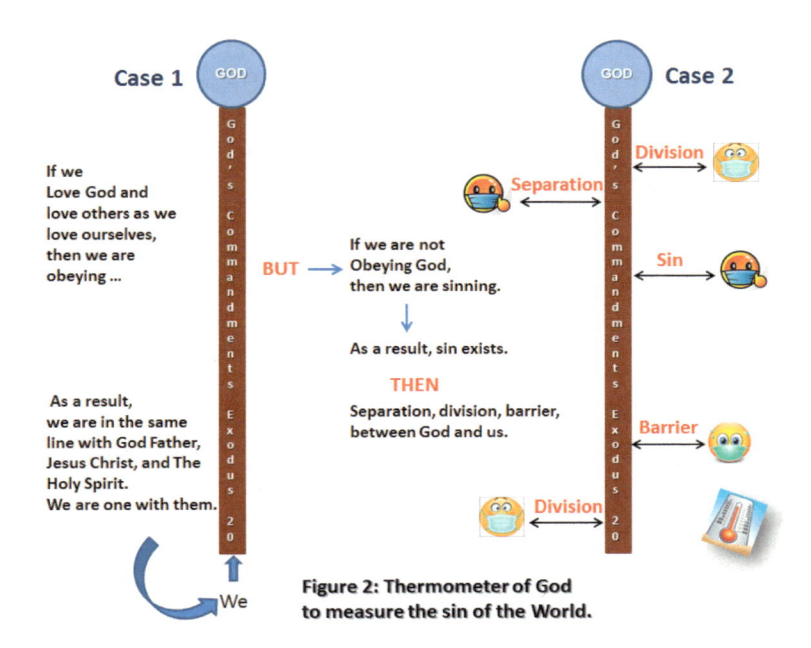

Figure 2: Thermometer of God to measure the sin of the World.

Case 1: If we Love God and love others as we love ourselves, then we are obeying ... **BUT** If we are not Obeying God, then we are sinning. As a result, sin exists. **THEN** Separation, division, barrier, between God and us.

As a result, we are in the same line with God Father, Jesus Christ, and The Holy Spirit. We are one with them.

Case 2: Division, Separation, Sin, Barrier, Division.

Jesus Christ is our hope. He is our saviour. He had an enormous assignment. He went through a painful and humiliating process to make our own lives easier, so we can finish as victorious. He came as the Lamb of God. He came for love to God and us. It was His starting point in His process. Then, during His life, He received love, respect, loyalty, envy, persecution, treason, humiliation, loneliness, favor, compassion, and death. Each person gave Him what they had inside them. It is the same with us. We will give others what we have inside us. We will receive from others what they have inside them. Jesus Christ was showing us part of the process of our life. *But also,* He showed us the Victory. When we obey, trust, and believe in God despite our circumstances, we pass each process of our life. Jesus was Holy without sin, but He suffered because He was taking our place to give us the strength and the peace to carry out God's plan.

Colossians 2: 13-15 mentions the victory of Jesus Christ. He cancelled the record of charges against us and took them away by nailing them to the cross. In this way, He disarmed the spiritual rulers and authorities. He shamed them publicly by His victory over them on the cross. The devil thought he was destroying God and Jesus when people were betraying, humiliating, beating, and crucifying Him; however, even when Jesus was suffering a lot, He was on His way to victory. He was disarming the enemy. How? If for God it is important to save our souls and lives, for the devil it is important that our souls be lost. In other words, while God wants eternal life and heaven for us, the devil wants the life and soul of people destroyed. It is the eternal death and hell. Sin produces it, but for God, the blood of Jesus Christ cleans away the sins. God allows our process because He wants to order our lives. He wants to save our souls. We must know what is coming from God or what is coming from the enemy.

Test vs. Temptation

The tests and temptations are part of a process. Our victory in that period of our life will depend on how strong our relationship is with God.

The tests come from God. It is like a school test that allows us to get to the next level. Here is our next spiritual level. It must be done because it is a promotion from God. It is for His Kingdom. So it is about people. It is about representing God and Jesus here on the Earth. Those tests most of the time are painful and demanding because they mainly work in our hearts. It requires people to move from their comfort zones to an unknown one, clean their minds, and renew their minds, hearts, life, and so on. Also, it includes attacks from the devil. Those are the obstacles and falls we must destroy and pass through to continue on our path.

The scripture says in James 1 that we should be happy when we have all kinds of tests because it proves our faith. I agree with that. We must increase our time with God during the process time. A benefit is that it will allow us to develop our mercy and compassion for ourselves and for others who would hurt or disappointment us. Then we are able to forgive and love them. The result of this is that the ties and traps of the enemy will be destroyed. Some recommendations to keep firm as the army of God before, during, and after tests and temptations include:

Reading His Word and other blessed books from real men and women of God, praying, fasting, worshiping, loving our family, helping more people, serving at the church, and sharing with the right people is one way to get to the next step and level of our lives.

Every day we must protect ourselves from the enemy's attacks. The apostle Paul said in Ephesians 6:10, 11, 17,18 (NKJV): "Be strong in the Lord and in the power of His might. Put on the whole Armor of God, which you may be able to stand against the wiles of the devil. Take the helmet of salvation, and the sword of the Spirit, which is the word of God; praying always with all prayer and supplication in the Spirit." It gives us our mind renewed with the Word of God. We receive the mind of Jesus Christ.

On the other hand, temptation comes from the enemy. It is all that makes people sin. Our mind is where it attacks often. Thoughts of condemnation, discrimination, disobedience, treason, hate, and fear are sown by the enemy. It is not coming from God. So, if we are in a deep relationship with God Father, Son, and Holy Spirit, we are far away from temptation. Otherwise, people open doors to temptation from the enemy. As a result, they live in sin. For example, drugs, drunkenness, disobedience, bitterness, wild parties, division, stealing, killing, selfish ambition, envy, idolatry, impurity, immorality, jealousy, lustful pleasures, excessive eating, etc. It guides people to act in the wrong way. It guides in an opposite direction from God, and the same direction of the devil. It leads to the traps of the devil. It is the desire of the flesh. It is sin.

To illustrate the traps of the enemy, I am going to share here some real cases. See the attached Figures 3a, 3b. I took this in July 2020 while writing this book. I am illustrating it with the Word of God to show you that God is always talking to us, but when people are far away from Him and do not pray, they cannot see what God is saying.

I usually had to cross to the other side of the road in that place. At the end of 2019 and beginning of 2020, some beautiful and flowery short trees were in that place. I illustrate it with the red circle in the picture. Those trees made it hard to view when cars were coming, so I could not check adequately. I realized it was a dangerous area. Those trees interrupted the visibility of the avenue crossing. Then I started to pray and ask God about whom I could inform about it, and I found the answer. The trees were cut sometime after I reported it, but it was in June-July when that place showed what God wanted to show us. Something that apparently is harmless can be used by the enemy to destroy. Why? You might ask. The picture might show you that it is just a place that is renewing its garden. However, God is showing us the result of praying for everything. A few months after praying, that area was dry and also showed something like a snake there. I know what I saw and reported, and I prayed for that place. I understood this as evident proof of how the enemy works. What was God instructing me to tell you? *Behind something that looks beautiful, harmless, perfect, and innocent, if you do not pray, you cannot see the giant and lethal snake hiding there.* Those are the traps of the enemy. Of course it is how the enemy works. Jeremiah 1:11-12 (NKJV) says: "Moreover the word of the Lord came unto me, saying, Jeremiah, what do you see? And I said, I see a branch of an almond tree. Then the Lord said to me, You have seen well, for I am ready to perform My word" *The secrets of God are just for those who spend time in secret with Him.*

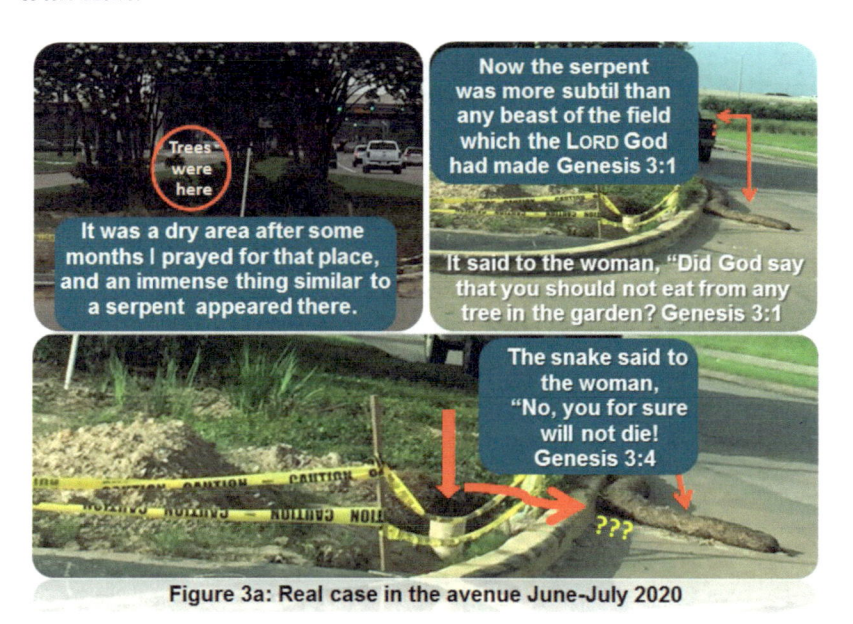

Figure 3a: Real case in the avenue June-July 2020

Chapter 7: Process

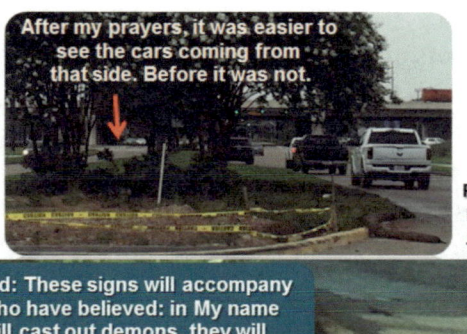

Figure 3b: Real case in the avenue June-July 2020

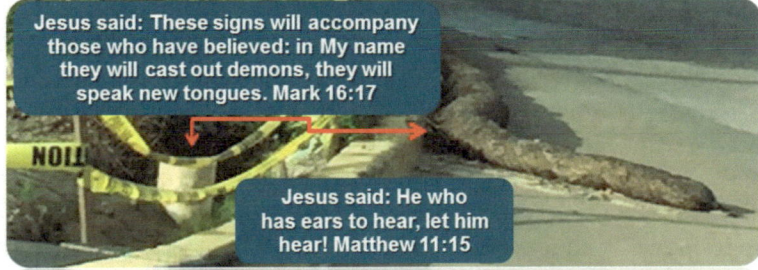

After my prayers, it was easier to see the cars coming from that side. Before it was not.

Jesus said: These signs will accompany those who have believed: in My name they will cast out demons, they will speak new tongues. Mark 16:17

Jesus said: He who has ears to hear, let him hear! Matthew 11:15

People must wake up to see our origin. We depend on God. He created us with a purpose, and to achieve it we must obey His will, not our will. However, people have lost their orientation. Our Father's Prayer says, "Your will be done here on the earth as it is in heaven," but it is not happening. There is a lot of sin. People might be doing it consciously or unconsciously, but the result is that sin is growing in the hearts of people and in the heart of the earth.

The main reason for a process is that God starts to take away from us all the impurities we have gotten from the world (society, leaders, people, etc.) who really do not know Him. It is individual, but the noise of the world speaks to how much sin exists in total humanity. So people who apply the weapon of God will keep firm, faithful, and without fear during their individual or a global process. We enter into a fire oven at this time. It is like Daniel and his friend when they were sent to the fire oven, but they were saved because God was with them. It is the same with us. If we seek God, if we go into His presence, if we obey Him, then we will pass the test. Some delicious food must be cooked into an oven at high temperature, and the result is a delicious, tasty, and fragrant food for our table. A process might be compared with an oven, when our character is cooked. The result of that is a spiritually mature person with a strong foundation, like a skyscraper or deep strong roots of a tree.

Our life is similar to a race. It is a journey with an exit and end point. Between those points, there is a path we must walk or run. If we want to win, we have to train. In my case, the challenges lived since I was a child through to adulthood have been part of the path I had to walk in order to detect what I had to change, improve, leave, avoid, fight against, keep, learn, and teach. Each tribulation lived can be taken as a training area, in my opinion, and experience. We can compare this with an iceberg. It is an immense block of ice where the bigger part is under the ocean. This is another way to compare our process with the strong foundations of a skyscraper, or the strong and deep roots of flourishing trees. Why? Because no one sees all the tribulations, faith, pain, suffering, sacrifice, obedience, work, denial, discipline, cleanliness, etc., that we must live in order to pass a process. There is an immense amount of hard work that must be done if we want to know our purpose and get the promises that God has told us. God is not seeking a perfect person. He seeks a contrite and humiliated heart, where He can work in people who allow Him to transform them into their origin.

Part of aunt Dai's process was my process as well. It was not easy for me to see her suffering. I was suffering as well. Some of the family supported her a lot, but I got the hardest part since the start of that aggressive cancer. It was the will of God. It was a painful and double process. Her pain was mine also. To me, it was unexplainable how that cancer made her belly grow so much in less than one month the third time it appeared. Each day it grew more and more. It was like a pregnancy of more than seven months. She could not walk well, she could not eat well, and she could not sleep well.

She passed away at the hospital. After her second surgery, her immune system was low, so the doctor ordered a blood transfusion before the chemotherapy. Each day we had to go to the hospital for her blood transfusion. It was painful for her when she was receiving it. That day I went early to buy fish for her, and I was looking for more blood donors. We got blood because my cousin helped us at the hospital, but I had to return the blood, so I was looking for new donors that day. When I arrived in the apartment, I saw her flip-flops between the bathroom and the hall of her bedroom. My heart started to speed up. She was on her bed. She told me, *"Jacke mija, me cai" ("Jacke mija, I fell.")* She was almost crying. It was the third time I saw her crying. The first time was the day of her birthday. We were still at the hospital after her second surgery. I bought her a beautiful and delicious cake, and some friends including two kind nurses were with her sharing that moment. She could not walk yet, so she was sitting in the wheelchair. While we were singing happy birthday, she was crying like a kid. It was a silent cry with her face almost hidden with the bedsheet. We all told her "do not cry" and hugged her. But, we all had our hearts broken and we were crying "inside". The second time I saw her crying was when she fell at the therapy center. When the cancer was returning again, her leg was affected again too, so she was receiving therapy to improve it. We went there every morning. One morning, she went out of the car to enter the center while I parked. From the distance, I saw when she fell. Some people helped her while I parked. When I entered the therapy center, I hugged her, and I was caressing her. She was crying like a kid in silence again, a lot of tears coming from her eyes, and a lot of questions in her eyes I could see. It deeply hurt me. For the first time in my life, I looked at my aunt crying. That time she was not hiding her face. Her face and her eyes were showing questions like, why was this happening to her? She did not understand why it was happening; why that aggressive sickness was in her. I was suffering with her. I did not understand either why that cancer came back again.

When she told me that she fell, I was almost crying, but I kept strong. I did not want to cry in front of her. Then I told her that we had to prepare to go to the hospital. I heard how she was losing her voice. I asked her why she was talking like that. And she told me, "I do not know." I was losing strength, hope, and faith. Even when I had talked with God about her two days before, inside I hoped that she could be healed. I helped her to dress. Then we went to pick up my cousin. When we were on our way to the hospital, Dai could not speak well, so we told her not to speak. I was praying to God to allow us to arrive at the hospital and keep her alive. When we arrived, my cousin took her in the wheelchair while I was parking. When I arrived in the observation room, other patients were there. Dai sat in the wheelchair. While I was talking with the doctor, a person told us she was not breathing well. She was turning purple, and then other doctors came.

They started to give her first aid. I was there desperately praying for help from God; others were praying as well. I saw how she was trying to survive. She wanted to live. Then the doctors told me to wait outside. I was praying and crying outside.

A few minutes after, the doctor came out and told me that she had died. When she told me that, it was as if someone had hit me. It was as if I was in a boxing ring during all that time I was with her during that sickness. Then when I heard the doctor, I felt I was knocked in that boxing ring. It was almost the same sensation I had when I quit my job. At that moment, I felt as if during my entire professional career, I were crossing a storm in the ocean with sharks around me. I fought off the storm and the sharks. However, despite all my effort, I reached the shore empty-handed and defeated. It was similar to my job with my beloved aunt. I gave my hope, my love, my dedication, my faith, and my obedience to God. However, she still died. I felt my hands were empty. I felt lost and defeated again. I went to the room and hugged and asked her why she left me. I asked her, "¿Qué le digo a Abuelita ahora, qué le digo a todos ahora si yo te estaba cuidando para regresarte sana y bella. ¿Cómo llego a la casa de Abuelita sin ti? ¿Cómo te voy a llevar sin vida? ¿Por qué me hiciste esto?" ("What am I going to tell now to Abuelita? What am I going to tell now to everybody when I was taking care of you to take you back home healthy and beautiful? How do I arrive at Abuelita's house without you? How will I take you there without life? Why did you do this to me?") I was crying, hugging, and asking her all those things.

After her funeral, I traveled back to my apartment. It was quite spacious without her. She was missing. I ate the same food she ate. I felt strange buying food that I used to eat before. I was just crying and feeling guilty. I thought I could do more for her. One morning, I called the sister of a loved friend who'd also passed away from cancer one year before. I asked her if I could have done something more for my aunt. And she told me that they did all they could do for my friend, and they also felt guilty. However, they then understood that nothing more was in their hands. I felt better. However, I did not want to pray. The Holy Spirit talked to me through different people in different places, and He told me that I had to stop the sadness. Clearly, He told me, "You cannot go with extra bags where you are going because the door is narrow." I understood the Holy Spirit was telling me I had to keep strong. I was moving to the U.S.A., another country totally different from mine, and to do what He was sending me there to do, I must avoid sadness and depression. It is so for everybody who wants to continue their path. We must find our strength in God if we want to continue. Otherwise, we fall into toxic emotions or beliefs that stop our purpose. It is sin, too. Matthew 7:13-14 (AMP) says: "Enter through the narrow gate. For wide is the gate and broad and easy to travel is the path that leads the way to destruction and eternal loss, and there are many who enter through it. But small is the gate and narrow and difficult to travel is the path that leads the way to [everlasting] life, and there are few who find it." At present, a lot of people are walking through the wide gate that is full of sin; they ought to repent from sins and come back to the path of God, the narrow door. I will talk more about it ahead.

After I received that word from the Holy Spirit, I asked God for strength. Then I started to pray again but not as before. My life was praying, worshiping, fasting, reading the Bible, but after my beloved aunt died, this decreased.

> *"Each one of us has moments of the desert. Those are the process's moments. To win and keep firm during those seasons, we must worship God. Then, to worship will become part of our daily food, as prayer is, too." –*
>
> *—Jackeline Alfonzo*

I started to worship with my grandmother when I was a child. However, it was just at church. But worship is not just singing. It is sung with our heart, mind, and soul. Also, worship is thanking God for everything. So this is how I have been living since I was a child. It comes from inside us, from our hearts. I thank Him for all. Even for the bad situations because I was learning that those storms were making me strong and helping me to grow spiritually.

I started a new level of worshiping the Lord when I spent some vacation days in Cape Town. I went to a bookstore there. I bought two CDs, one for Christmas and another totally new for me. It had amazing songs to God. When I came back to Angola, every morning when I was going to the office, I used to worship. Each morning when I was singing, I was crying. It was spontaneous. The tears were out of my eyes alone. Our flesh might not know what it is, but our spirit totally understands it when it is done sincerely and from our heart. The Holy Spirit was touching my heart, and I did not know it at the time.

Worshiping the Lord has been the vitamin for my heart and spirit. It also opens the doors of heaven each time I do it. It is talking in another way with God the Father, Son, and the Holy Spirit. I did not have enough time to cry for Dai or for Abuelita when they left. I was still crying about Dai's death when suddenly Abuelita also died. I thought I could not continue because I did not have the strength. One night I was crying a lot for Abuelita while I was worshiping the Lord God, so I cried out to God to help me. I had to keep strong to do what God was asking and to continue with my English classes. It was what He asked me to do as soon as I came to the USA. I could not come here with extra bags that were sadness, depression, or other feelings. The next morning I had the strength, and I could continue doing my best in my classes. Everything is always in order. While I have been writing this book, it is inevitable to miss my beloved aunt, grandmother, even my family who are in Venezuela. So, in some way, writing has been allowing me to heal my heart. It is like a wound that was not well healed but needs to be healed. A doctor has to open that wound and clean it. In this way was my heart. I had wounds in my heart that needed healing. Jesus opened my heart, and He was healing me. He is our healer. We are victorious in our processes even when we do not understand why things are happening. To obey and walk in the purpose of God is another way to worship Him. So, during your process, during your desert, even though you do not have strength, do what the Lord asks of you.

> *"The Lord said: 'Let My people go,*
> *that they may hold a feast to Me in*
> *the wilderness. Let My people go, that*
> *they may serve Me in the*
> *wilderness.'"*
>
> *—Exodus 5:1 & 7:16 NKJV*

CHAPTER 8

Purpose

"The Purpose is a beginning and an end. It is a vision and a path. It is a true north, a focus. It is a goal, an achievement. It is a search, an encounter. It is to fall but to rise again. It is time and patience. It is love and a reason. It is mind, heart, and soul. It is mercy, service, and compassion. It is blood even though other people cannot see it. It is blood in our tears, blood on our knees, and blood in our hearts. It is a sincere smile and peace in the middle of a storm because we believe even when other people cannot see what we see. It is to speak, to listen, and to obey. It is joy, grace, and favor. It is Jesus Christ, our Rock."

—Jackeline Alfonzo.

In the chapter on Process, I wrote about how we have a start and end point. We find several options during our journey on earth. However, God's purpose for us is the right path. We find it when we want to please Him, and we are in His presence to clearly listen to His voice and His instructions. Isaiah 44:1-2 (AMP) says: "But now listen, O Jacob, my servant, and Israel, whom I have chosen: This is what the Lord who made you and formed you from the womb, who will help you says, *'Fear not, O Jacob My servant; And Jeshurun (Israel, the upright one) whom I have chosen.'"* To receive God's purpose, we must totally trust in Him even when we see the opposite from what He has told us. A short definition of purpose is, the intention of doing or not doing something, or the goal that we would like to obtain in our life. Myles Munroe in his book *The Spirit of Leadership* defined it like this: *"The discovery of a reason for its existence, and it is the original intention of creating a thing."* In the case of God, He created the earth and the human being, so He has a reason with His creation, and we must value it. Then it is our responsibility to find our own. How do we find it? We have to be servants of God instead of servants of sin. The servant might sound like slave, but people will really become slaves depending on their choices. I see clearly how Isaiah 44 shows that the Word of God is alive. It is the same as yesterday, today, and forever. At present, who is God referring to when He said, "O Jacob My servant" and "And Jeshurun (Israel, the upright one)"? He is referring to everybody who is His servant and His Israel. It is everybody who has been born again in Jesus Christ. Therefore, as God includes instead of excludes, He is calling to the rest of His servants and Israelites missing in His Kingdom.

A definition of servant is, a person who performs duties for others, especially a person employed in a house for domestic duties. That person receives a salary for their work. However, Jesus taught us who truly is a servant of God. In Matthew 20:25-28 (NLV), He called His disciples to Him and said: *"You know how the kings of the nations show their power to the people. Important leaders use their power over the people. It must not be that way with you. But whoever wants to be great among you, let him care for you. For the Son of Man came not to be cared for. He came to care for others."* At present, in nations, institutions, organizations, churches, and so on, they are missing a real and genuine service and leadership. The main cause is because there is no real and honest relationship of love with God. The identity in Jesus Christ is missing. Jesus came to save us, but He also came to teach us what service really is and who God's servants really are.

The scripture says that our hearts plan our way, but it is the Lord who directs our steps. So, our purpose is not discovered when people who are far away from God inform us. It is not told by our parents, though they must pray and guide us. It is not told by our friends or our shepherds. They help us and support us in prayer when we are in a church that cares for its people, but it is our responsibility to stay in secret with God. We have to stay in a deep relationship with the Trinity, which is Father, Son, and the Holy Spirit, to know that amazing purpose God entrusted us with. However, today, we can see how people have been allowing others to manage their lives according to their own convenience. We can see how people live according to their flesh and passions. When we understand with an open heart that we are to be instructed and taught by God and the people God sends to us, and we are to instruct and teach the people God sends us, we find our purpose in the middle of the desert. If we keep worshiping, praying, fasting, persisting, and serving our Lord God, then we are on the path to find our purpose.

The book of Esther in the Bible is an example of how our plan is the plan God has for us.

She was a Jewish maiden who became the queen of Persia. Even when she was a simple girl, she had a tremendous destiny and purpose for her life. She did not know about that, but God was guiding her. Esther was an orphan; she was adopted and educated by her cousin Mordecai. Even though she was Jewish, she became the queen of Persia because the king selected her. Her right behaviour, obedience, and favor from God gave her that important position. As a result, she saved her nation and her adoptive father when a group of people were planning to destroy and exterminated them. She was not prepared to talk to the king, her husband about that situation. However, her cousin told her: *"For if you remain completely silent at this time, relief and deliverance will arise for the Jews from another place, but you and your father's house will perish. Yet who knows whether you have come to the kingdom for such a time as this?" Esther 4:14 (NKJV)*. On her own strengths, she did not have the bravery or solutions to do that. Then she proclaimed three days of fasting with all the Jews. As a result, she received confirmation, guidance, instruction, courage, and wisdom from God, and she saved her cousin and her nation. It is the same with us. In our own strengths and will, we cannot do what God has assigned us to do. On my own strengths, I could not walk the path of the process of my beloved aunt. It was with the forces of God that I could, but also in the church was an army of men and women of God supporting her and me with their prayers.

I did not know what the next step of God's plan for me was until I had to finally write a book. It was one of the first things God showed me when He opened my spiritual eyes in 2015. He showed me that I had to write. However, I was not thinking about a book. I was writing what I was learning from the Bible. But the more I am in the presence of the Lord and the more I obey Him, the more I discover what He is asking me to do. It has not been easy, but God opens the way when we are calling on Him and depending on Him. Each place we go with the instructions of God is part of our purpose. For this reason, we ought to pray to God to know where He wants us.

The church that we attend also forms part of God's plan. We should pray to Him, asking for direction as to the church He wants us to attend. This was my experience when I was telling Him I wanted to know more, and I wanted to know more about why some things happened to me, my family, and on the Earth. As a result, He sent me where I started to get answers. In 2015, in Venezuela, the church my friend invited me to was my school. All my questions started to get answers, and I started my deep and true relationship with God Father, Jesus Christ, and the Holy Spirit. My life started to be founded on our Rock, Jesus Christ. Then, the Holy Spirit promoted me to the university. It was the university of English and the university of my next church to be planted. Now was the time to show all He had been teaching me.

As I mentioned before, in August 2018 when I came to the U.S., my first plan was to study English to improve it. I decided to live near the college where I was studying. I did not want to drive on the freeway in Houston. I was not prepared. I wanted to attend the Lakewood Church, but it and the college are located in opposite directions, so even when I tried to go to service, I was not able to. I used to get ready to go, and when I'd just opened the door to leave, I started to feel nervous, and I found any excuse to stay. Additionally, I was not familiar with GPS, so that was not helping me with the decision to go. I had some weeks without attending a church even though I was committed and it was an important part of my life. I knew that God's plan was to continue what He started with me, so I kept praying He would lead me to where He wanted me to go.

Then I started to attend a church located less than ten minutes from where I lived. In the first service, I got an answer to a question I used to ask God about why Dai died. It thought, "God is Sovereign, and sometime there is not an answer to why things happen." In the next service, when the sermon finished, one person told me, *"I see you preaching there soon,"* and he pointed to their pulpit. That might be a comment for someone who is expecting a pulpit, but not for me. I just wanted what God wanted for me. So I continued praying to God, asking if this was the church He wanted me to attend. Then the next Sunday when I woke up, I said to Him: *"I am not sure if that is the church, but I will go because I told you I will go again this week to be sure if it is."* When I looked at my cell phone, I had a message from a friend. She wrote to me that in the name of God our Father and Father of Jesus Christ, I had to go to Lakewood (LW) that Sunday at 2:00 p.m., and it would be for good. She did not know I was praying and asking direction from God about which church He wanted me in. Only He knew about my prayer. So when I read that message, I started to pray asking God to guide me and protect me on my way to the church. My hands started to sweat, which is not common, but I was so nervous because I knew it was an order from Him. So the excuses and fear of not going to LW ended. I knew that I had to go even if I did not understand the GPS or was afraid to drive on the freeway. I saw that God was calling me there, so I had to go.

On my way, I decided to drive toward the avenue. It was slow, and the clock was ticking. Then I knew that I had to take courage and drive on the freeway. It was scary, but I did it. A lot of immense cars were there near me driving at high velocity. The air conditioning was on, but my hands were sweating. However, the Holy Spirit led me with verses of the Scripture. I was speaking them while I was driving. Finally, I arrived on time at the church. When the worship finished, the shepherd said he felt a special presence of the Holy Spirit. Then he started to minister to the volunteers of the church because the Holy Spirit told him to. He called over the volunteers of the church. However, I took that call, too, because even though I was not yet a volunteer there, I said that I was a volunteer for God everywhere. Additionally, the Holy Spirit asked me to go there, so for me, this was a date He'd made with me. The Holy Spirit was talking to me directly. After that, I immediately applied to serve at the church. I thought I could take a break after my beloved aunt died, but God wanted me to continue. The only reason why I drove the freeway those first few months was to attend the church, and I used to get nervous. Several times, I missed the right exit or entry, or I took the wrong one, but it did not stop me; instead, it strengthened me.

I had to overcome new challenges sometime after I started to attend the church. It was a drastic change for me. I was coming from a church where we were always in contact with our leaders, pastors, disciples, and little sheep. I was starting everything again. I was far away from my family again. I was still deeply hurt for Dai, and also, I had to start creating a new family in Christ. Honestly, I felt like I was in a car without a seatbelt at that new church. I was in an immense place with a lot of people and pastors, but I did not have anyone to talk to or ask to pray directly for me because I was not familiar with them. I used to stay in contact with my leaders and pastors at the previous church, but I knew I had to stop because God had sent me to that new one, and they were my new family in Christ. Then I started to attend a Spanish life group. Also, the church called me to start my training as an usher at the English service.

Additionally, I started to pray, asking God for some people who would support me through prayer. Then a few months later, when I was ushering, a kind person told me that I had showed fidelity with my service at the church, and I had opened doors there. That person asked me for my petitions for prayer. So I saw it as an answer from God for someone to support me through praying. "My petitions are huge and might look crazy for people, but it is what I am praying for." I wrote this to that person when I was writing out my prayers. The answer was something like, if I saw it in my spirit, I would have it because it was a desire that God put inside me. That amazing answer gave me hope.

Shortly thereafter, the Holy Spirit showed me in different ways that I had to apply for a job at the church and volunteer with the kids. I prayed a lot, asking for direction, because this never was in my plan, but He led me to do this several times. *So one plus one equals two.* All was looking like it was matching with what the person at the church had told me about opening doors. But it was not like that. God does not work as we would. I started to apply, but I got closed doors. I applied for different job positions opened at the church, but I was rejected, and *surprise!* For the first time in my service life to God at

His temples since 2015, I was not accepted as a volunteer. I easily could see in my first interview that I was not welcome there. I said, ok, maybe I understood God wrong to apply there. However, He showed me in different ways that I had to try again, and I did. Then I found obstacles regarding the security rules of the church to apply to that service. So I told God that I did not understand, but from my side, I did not want to try again because I did not want to force anything regarding service unless He told me again.

Then God wanted to turn up the heat, so He did. One Sunday, a famous singer was a guest of the church, so days before, additional volunteers were asked for the performance. As usual, I sent my name in to help. I was doing this with each event where it was needed. *Surprise again!* That Sunday when I was serving in the morning, I was told that I was not chosen to serve at the event coming up that night because security would not allow me to volunteer at that event. Then I felt an immense pain cutting and traversing through my heart. I could not believe what I was hearing. But this was the decision. That afternoon, my volunteer supervisors were trying to let me attend that event, *but the security said no.* I thanked my team leaders for that, and I told them that if I was not allowed to stay there, it was because God did not want me to attend that event. It was not the will of the security people. And because I am a prayer Intercessor, I said that this was another way to serve the church. I went to the apartment to pray for that event and all the people there. After I prayed, I became exhausted and went to sleep for a little bit. Then the great and wonderful blessing and love of God came that same night when I woke up. It was early at night yet, so a few seconds after I woke up, a guitar started playing. God sent me a serenade. From my bedroom, I could hear it. It was the song "Way Maker" with a guitar. I started to cry because "Way Maker" is a promise in Isaiah 43:16-19 He gave me at the beginning of my new life with Him. It says: "Thus says the Lord, who makes a way in the sea and a path through the mighty waters, brings forth the chariot and horse the army and the power. Do not remember the former things, nor consider the things of old. Behold, now it shall spring forth; shall you not know it? I will do a new thing. I will even make a road in the wilderness and rivers in the desert." He was talking clearly to me. He knew the wounds in my heart because of what happened, but He was reminding me that He is who opens doors, and He is our way maker. He was reminding me that the fight is with the devil, who tries to make us surrender our purpose. He was reminding me of when He was with the Israelites when He opened the red sea to allow them to walk through, and then when He destroyed the pharaoh along with his army. He does the same for us. He was reminding me that I do not have to worry about anything because He is God, who deeply loves me and fights for me. And, like me, He deeply loves you and fights for you. We must trust during our tests; otherwise, we are not able to continue our purpose until we are prepared.

Some days after, I prayed to God asking if this really was the church that He wanted for me or if I understood wrong. I wanted to be sure. Then He answered that I had to stay there. I could not move. It was where He sent me. By that time, I was in a deep time of fasting, praying, worshiping, and reading His Word. The Holy Spirit had led me to do that some weeks before. He was showing me more that I had to write a book. But also, attacks from the enemy in my mind started. I was receiving memories about past moments I'd lived when I was working. After I quit and started my real relationship with God, I asked Him for a balanced life where He would be first. I used to ask Him how I was going to have a balanced life taking classes, writing the book, working, helping my family and other people. How could I help the young adults in my country and other places where I have seen them without hope and faith? How could I go to the schools, colleges, and universities to talk about the immense and wonderful love You have for all of us and help them? How could I encourage people and tell them that they can be better people if they allow Jesus Christ and the Holy Spirit to lead their lives? How could I get a balanced life with all You have sown in my heart, but without interrupting nor decreasing my relationship with You? Also, how am I going to build an ark? In the middle of 2019 clearly, He asked me to build an ark.

I did not understand what He meant when He said I had to build an Ark. I did not know how to put together all God was asking me without affecting my moments with Him. Then I started to mention the book to some people asking for help, but I did not get answers. I knocked on the doors of some expert writers in Spanish asking for help with the book, but I only heard *silence and/or unrealistic ways of writing a book*. Let's not forget that our service to others brings blessings to our lives and makes God smile. There are people who just want to take your time, energy, focus..., but there are others who really need help. Let's be watchful to see on whose faces we might paint a smile, or even save their life only with a word, gesture, answer, or a hug. Let's give others some of the blessings of abilities, knowledge, time, love, and attention that God has given us. The rushes, pride, indifference, individualism, narcissism, selfishness, egocentrism, and so on are some of the reasons why God is allowing confinement. With the social distancing, God is letting us know this is what exists inside people. A barrier of sin and vanities is separating and degrading the love and mercy among people and God. The only way to solve this is by spending time in secret with Him. The world needs less sin and less life in the flesh. It needs more time with God and more life in the spirit. Then we become more merciful, helpful, kind, and loving, with ourselves and with others.

I solved what I was looking for because I was led by the Holy Spirit and the prayers of my family, the church, and myself. The Holy Spirit was guiding me at each event I had to go through at the church because what I needed was there, but I had to find it. It was like a rally, a car race where we have to find some hidden questions or clues needed to arrive at our final station. He sent me to the church He wanted at even when it was apparently in opposition. Part of what I needed was there, but I saw it a few times when I was asked for my list of petitions for prayers. My eyes were opened. I saw in the bulletin of information for the church about the business conferences done each month. I did not see them before. Then I started to attend. In that place, I found who was leading me toward the book.

During her presentation, I heard two bold words: *transition and balanced life*. It is for me, I said. I knew I was in a transition, where the potter Jesus Christ had destroyed my old life to build my new one. And I knew the new one was about the balanced life I had been asking God for, where He was first, then everything after. I knew I would get answers to what I was looking for from her. However, it did not happen immediately. I kept praying and fasting. Also, I continued trying to find a job. I was getting tired of writing resumes for each job application and getting rejected. I was tired of losing my time doing that. Then one night, while I was writing a new resume for a new job application, I was crying and asking God what He wanted from me. I was asking Him why He was sending me to do things where I was losing time, and it was hurting me more. *"God, what do you want from me?"* I asked Him. Then suddenly, I got an email from the person

I'd met at the conference. Some days later, we had our meeting, and, as always, God gave me more than I was expecting. She was able to guide me with the book. This was how I closed in on 2019. I knew that the door to starting the book, which was the Ark God was asking of me, was opened in 2020 to fulfill God's assignment to me.

To conquer our purpose, we had better stay in a deep relationship with God. God Father, Son, and the Holy Spirit will never leave us alone.

> *"Blessed are those who die in the Lord from now on. Yes, says the Spirit, they are blessed indeed, for they will rest from their hard work; for their good deeds follow them!"*
>
> *—Revelation 14:13 (NLT)*

Sometimes our purpose might look like a relay race. This was what The Holy Spirit showed me one morning while I was serving at the church. One person does his/her part, and then the relay baton goes to other hands. It happened with Dai and I. She gave me the relay baton when she left because she did not have the opportunity to stay alive and enjoy her family, but she knew her testimony might help others. She was a passionate woman who loved all that she did. And even when it was a hard job or task, she did it with love, passion, and dedication. She opened her heart to the potter, Jesus Christ, to allow Him to clean it, heal it, and save her soul. She would speak about it if she were alive, but she is not. However, God allowed me to write a little about her life because she left me the relay baton.

> *"My sheep hear My voice, and I know them, and they follow Me."*
>
> *— John 10:27 (NKJV)*

To find and to make true the plan of God in us, we must look for it and follow it without stopping despite the adversities we might find. We must stay in the blessing's promises. Regrets go against our purpose, so we must eliminate them from our life. Our first purpose from God is to increase and expand His Kingdom, and His Kingdom is about people. He wants all His children there, and we need Jesus Christ to form part of the family of God.

Chapter 8: Purpose

In 2012, I attended a geology course, and the whole class traveled to Pyrenees, Spain. My first morning at the hotel, I woke up to the sound of a belt. And when I looked out the windows...*Wow!* It was a shepherd with his little sheep. This was my first time seeing that.

Figure 1

Then that same day, the gifts from God continued with the extraordinary nature of that blessed place. Also, He spoke to me in His supernatural way, but I did not understand at that time. When we were near the mountains, we listened to a little sheep. She was alone, and she was lost. She might be crying for someone to help her. This might be what God, the only one who can see our hearts, saw in Dai, my family, and me. However, I could not understand Him. I did not know I was one of the lost sheep of Jesus Christ, and He was calling me to really know Him, to take care of my family and me.

Jesus Christ asked His disciple:

What do you think about this? A man has one hundred sheep and one of them is lost. Will he not leave the ninety-nine and go to the mountains to look for that one lost sheep? Matthew 18:12 (NLV)

I was one of His lost sheep

Figure 2

Jesus was calling me to teach me how to start that life I was dreaming of. *My dream life? A purposeful life. It is a life based on God's plan for us.* I see it as an immense building with strong foundations that none can destroy. I did not know that the *only* one who can give us that life is *Jesus Christ, our ROCK.*

Figure 3

Even though I was giving fruits, Jesus Christ called me. He wanted to teach me how to give the right fruits in the right Kingdom. He wanted me like a strong and green tree planted near rivers, where He is the water. He is the water I needed, and, like the Samaritan He went to encounter at the water well, He did so with me. Then after I found Him, I left the oil, gas, and water wells I was studying and taking care of, and He made me change wells for people. While people who were being processed by Him were taking care of me, and while I was in process, too, I started to take care of people who also needed Him. Finally, He wanted me to take off the helmet I thought was right for me, but it was just destroying me. Then He introduced me to the Holy Spirit, and the Holy Spirit gave and taught me how to wear the salvation helmet of the Armor of God. Then I stopped being a victim to become victorious.

Chapter 8: Purpose

Figure 4

Similar to me, Jesus Christ has been calling you, but the noise of your life does not allow you to listen or to understand Him. God is calling all His children to His Kingdom, but it is your choice. We are responsible for our choices. Your option today will include your children, the children of your children, and also the earth. So, to walk in the path and truth of God, we must listen to our main Shepherd, Jesus Christ. He said: "I am the Good Shepherd. I know My sheep and My sheep know Me. I know My Father as My Father knows Me. I give My life for the sheep. I have other sheep which are not from this sheep-pen. I must bring them also. They will listen to My voice. Then there will be one flock with one shepherd" John 10:14-16 (NLT). He wants all His little sheep on His path. From east to west and north to south of the world, Jesus is calling all of us.

Figure 5

Jesus asked His disciples in Matthew 16:15-18: "But who do you say that I am?" Simon Peter said, "You are the Christ, the Son of the living God." Jesus said to him, "Simon, son of Jonah, you are happy because you did not learn this from man. My Father in heaven has shown you this. And I tell you that you are Peter. On this rock, I will build my church." When Jesus said "On this rock I will build my church," He was referring to the rock of His revelation of the *Son of God* and obedience of His Word. So when we have that revelation from God, each one of us is like Peter, Paul, John, and so on. Each one of us stopped being a lost little sheep to start being a pure disciple of Jesus Christ. But first, you have to listen to His voice. And He is calling each one of His little sheep, each one of the prodigal sons of God, to come back to His Kingdom.

CHAPTER 9

Salvation

"Never forget where I got you from...your family, neighborhood, city...

Never forget where I got you from...your Secret Place.

May I never forget where you got me from, Lord of my life.

May I never forget that without YOU, my beloved, I am nobody.

May I never forget to be in your presence, Father of my life, my Lord, my Owner, my Teacher, my Potter, and my Shepherd.

Thank you for your love, my everything, my God...my Treasure."

—Jackeline Alfonzo

We are saved by the grace of God. Ephesians 2:8 (NLV) says that by His loving-favor, we have been saved from the punishment of sin through faith. *But faith in who? What gives us salvation?* The only one who gives us that salvation is Jesus Christ, the Son of God. Salvation is to have Him in our hearts because He was sent by God to give us access to the Throne of Grace of God and Eternal life. He is our *only great High Priest* who can give us that blessing. Romans 10:9 states (NLV): "If you say with your mouth that Jesus is the Lord, and believe in your heart that God raised Him from the dead, you will be saved from the punishment of sin." The principle of this confession is that we are saying: "I believe in you, Jesus Christ. I thank you for what you did for me on the cross. I thank your love and sacrifice for me, so from now on, I leave my old life to start a new one honoring and obeying your Word and commandments. I crucified my flesh and my own passions to do your will. I take my cross and offer you my life as you did for me." Salvation is to crucify our flesh and to do the will of God in us. It means we have to die to our old life.

Some people believe that life is here on Earth, and after that, all is over. However, I see life similar to a journey needed to win the promises of God and His promised Land, which is with Him in heaven. Whatever the reason for a journey—for example, business, pleasure, etc.—everybody prepares and wants to arrive safely to their destination. The same with our life here on earth. We ought to prepare our travel to heaven while living here. We must live according to the commandments of God. Our salvation starts while living instead of after death. Each one of us is responsible for protecting it. We ought to inform others *that salvation* will be lost when people do not obey what God has decreed in His Word. It might be lost when we live in sin. It is lost if we do not repent forever of our sins. 1 John 2:16-17 KJV: "For all that is in the world, the lust of the flesh, and the lust of the eyes, and the pride of life, is not of the Father, but is of the world. And the world passed away, and the lust thereof: but he that doeth the will of God abideth forever."

If you do not believe in Jesus Christ as the Son of God, which god do you believe in? The Bible is clear. It shows that salvation is equal to faith. God asked of us *faith*. But that *faith* ought to be in Him and His Word. In the past, God talked to His Prophets about His warnings to get His mercy or His anger, depending on our decisions. An evident example is Habakkuk, the prophet. He asked God: *"O Lord, how long shall I cry, and You will not hear? Even cry out to You, 'Violence!' and You will not save. Why do You show me iniquity, and cause me to see trouble? For plundering and violence are before me; there is strife, and contention arises."* Habakkuk 1:2-3 NKJV. The prophet was crying out to God for the injustices living at that time.

Today, when most people live without a care about what happens with humanity, or they believe there is not a healer for that worldwide cancer produced by sin; others are staying in the presence of God, talking to Him about the disorders, indifferences, injustices, and distortions in the World. Like Habakkuk, today, still God shows some people what is coming, and some people talk with God about the lie, cruelty, and abominations here. Today, there are some people with their voices known in heaven. Like in the past, God uses His watchtowers to observe the Earth. An earthly watchtower is an observation tower where a guard waits to alert about enemies or unexpected disasters. Like the armed forces of each country might have their sentries, God has His sentries located in His watchtowers, too. An earthly watchtower has to be in a high position to easily look at the whole horizon around him/her. However, a sentinel of God, while nearest, are his/her eyes and ears to the feet of Christ, the more they surrender their hearts to God, the more powerful is his/her spiritual vision and audition on Earth, and stronger his/her voice in Heaven. This is because his/her spirit is aligned with the Holy Spirit. So, in the present, it is easy for the sentinels of God to perceive, smell, and predict what is happening in their family, neighborhood, church, city, country, and the world, comparing it with the Scriptures and with the things the Holy Spirit says and shows them.

> ***"But if the watchman sees the sword come and blow not the trumpet, and the people be not warned; if the sword come, and take any person from among them, he is taken away in his iniquity; but his blood will I require at the watchman's hand."***
>
> *—Ezequiel 33:6 (KJV)*

In 2016, the Holy Spirit clearly showed me an airplane accident. As an intercessor, I started praying for each national and international worldwide flight, and I asked for support from the intercessor team at the church. After so many flights I took during my professional career, I was familiar with the sound of an airplane when it was taking off or landing. So, from my apartment, I spiritually heard that sound. Then I started hearing another strong sound coming from the air or sky. It was distant in the same line or parallel to the window of my bedroom, my watchtower by that time. It was repeated through the airplane's vision shown by the Holy Spirit. So I continually was hearing those sounds that I did not understand at the time. A few weeks after, I received a video with similar sounds reported there. Some were mentioned as the trumpets of God. It was not exactly the sound of earthly trumps. I would describe what I heard as the sound of ferries or roars in the sky. I told my shepherd at that time. Then some weeks later, I heard information about the flight accident of the Brazilian football team. It hurt me a lot. I was crying and asking God why it happened when I was praying during that time to protect all the flights, and I'd informed the church to pray, too. I felt guilty because I thought I did not pray enough. So I wrote again to the shepherd. She told me that I did not have to feel guilty because I did all I could do, and maybe that accident would have been worse and more people would have died.

With time, all receive the answers. We are in the last prophetic times. Jesus Christ will come to save His church, and all who believe and obey Him are part of His church. We are the body of Christ. God wants all of us in His kingdom. So, like when I asked the church to pray about what the Holy Spirit showed me, now He wants me to inform you through this book to repent and come back to God. Because it is His will and His time, I am informing you of what God has been teaching, showing, and asking me before and while I write. Like in the time of Noah, it is happening now. Genesis 6:11-12 KJV: "The earth also was corrupt before God, and the earth was filled with violence. And God looked upon the earth, and behold, it was corrupt; for all flesh had corrupted his way upon the earth." As in the past, some people have been creating and approving rules, and living according to those changes, instead of God's laws. It is an evident open door to the anger and judgment of God if it does not stop and change immediately.

> *"In those days they will no longer say, 'The fathers have eaten sour grapes, and the children got the sour taste.' But everyone will die for his own sin. Each man who eats the sour grapes will get the sour taste."*
>
> *—Jeremiah 31:29-30 (NLT)*

The families, friends, religious leaders, and so on ought to pray for themselves, their families, and one to another while they are alive instead of when a person dies to save their soul. Some religious people are not speaking the truth, and their congregants are at risk of not going to the presence of God. Also, I would say whoever is not teaching the truth of God is at risk of losing his/her salvation, too. God will ask all of us what we did with what He gave us, and it is a sin when we can do good, but we choose not to. We must protect our eternal life while we are here on Earth. If there is no repentance of sin before death, there is no salvation after death. If people do not believe in Jesus Christ as the Son of God nor the Holy Spirit, they are not saved.

Dai and I spent one month or so at the hospital after her second surgery. I said to myself that the enemy wanted me far away from the church, and he wanted to make my aunt suffer as well, so this was my opportunity to introduce Jesus Christ to all people who I was meeting at the hospital and in the street. Then I started to do it. Because of the difficult situation living in my country, the families of the patients had to buy all the medicines and surgery materials needed. So, each time I had to go out to do this, I used to stop in places where I could talk with people about the Bible and Jesus Christ. I was surprised because I met people who did not know the Bible.

Inside the hospital, I used to visit other sick people. In the bedroom next to where we were was a lovely grandma with her daughter who spent months at the hospital. The lovely grandma invited me to their bedroom to pray after I did it the first time. Some days after, her daughter started to improve, and she praised the Lord with us. She and her family accepted Jesus Christ. Her mother was happy. She was a cute grandma. She conquered my heart as an old grandma was strong taking care of her daughter. Even when her son-in-law used to visit his wife, the cute grandma was spending all that time with her daughter at the hospital. The night before the girl's surgery, I went to their room. It was lovely because other sick people were there. We all prayed and worshiped. It was a blessed moment. She had surgery the next day; however, very early the day after her surgery, we woke up because the grandma was screaming and crying. Her daughter had passed away while she was in the observation room. Dai and I woke up while the grandma was screaming, so I told Dai, "La abuela" (the grandma). Then I ran out of the bedroom to find her. She was crying and asking why she'd died. Why did this happen when she was feeling better? Why, if she was recovering her happiness, did she die? I was hurt as well. So I just was with her hugging, crying, and praying. I told her that in 1 Thessalonians 4:13-14 it says whoever sleeps in Christ will resurrect with Him. "But I do not want you to be ignorant, brethren, concerning those who have fallen asleep, lest you sorrow as others who have no hope. For if we believe that Jesus died and rose again, even so God will bring with Him those who sleep in Jesus." It was a sad moment for everyone on that floor in the hospital. I helped the grandma to collect all her things from the bedroom while she was waiting for her family. Then I walked with her to the exit to hug and say goodbye to her. Her pain was my pain. After that, I called my shepherdess at that time. She told me: "When you are in front of a sick person, just focus on his/her soul. You did what you had to do. She was saved."

The time to live after death is it. Save the soul of the people. The real life is eternal with God. But to get there, the souls of people must be healed and saved. This is done *only* by Jesus Christ. It is not about the body, it is about a saved soul. We save it when we allow Him to enter our heart and work in it. So, He cleans our heart of sin, and heals it of unforgiveness. With the wounds He received in His body and His heart, He heals our souls. Then our travel while we are here on Earth is light to us and pleasant to God. I am totally sure that the grandma at the hospital had prayed a lot for the recovery of her daughter, as I did for my beloved aunt. But she did not know the true healing and salvation is in our soul. Jeremiah 31:29-30 is clear; each one of us is responsible for our salvation. None can save others without the truth, and the truth is Jesus Christ is our *only* healer and savior. The truth is that we ought to repent of our sin forever and never more come back to it. The truth is that we ought to take our cross and honor, thank, and obey Jesus Christ; otherwise, hell is the destiny while living on Earth, and after death for the souls if there is not repentance and transformation.

> *"There are many rooms in My Father's house. If it were not so, I would have told you. I am going away to make a place for you. ³After I go and make a place for you, I will come back and take you with Me."*
>
> *—John 14:2-3 (NLV)*

When I accompanied Dai for one of her medical tests before her second surgery, she told me she did not want to come back to her house; she wanted a new place where she felt quiet and at peace. Because I had some land behind my mother's house, I asked her if she would like a small house there. She said yes. Then that small house was built. We went to buy some things for the house while we were in my apartment. I wanted to give the best I could for her. I wanted to make her feel loved. However, she could not enjoy it. But the plans of God are better than ours. We might not understand, but He knows more than us.

In 2019, my brother sent me a song because it reminded him of our aunt Dai. When I heard the song, I saw my own experience and my time with her. It is about a flower (woman) who was found on the road. She looked withered and lifeless; she was rejected and mistreated at her job. She looked almost pale, and she was without hope. However, she was taken to the garden of someone who found her, and she was saved. He was taking care of her with all his soul and all his love. Then she recovered her color, and she recovered her freedom because she was being taken care of properly.

Dai was a lover of children, arts, nature, and sowing. She had blessed hands to create, sow, and harvest surprisingly. She was fertile land to plant in, too. She wanted a life of peace. However, she was planting in her heart the wrong seeds of the world. She was allowing the devil to sow in her mind the wrong voices of its lies; it made her believe that she was not loved anymore by her mother or by her brothers. Because she did not know the complete truth of God, she was allowing the enemy to steal the seeds of God, and it stole her breath, her joy, and her peace. It was withering her heart, mind, and soul, but she did not know it. Then, one day it was reflected on the outside of her. We who deeply love her could see her pale face from an unexpected, silent, and deadly illness that was growing in her belly. I was with her during that painful process. That was processing me, too. I took her to my apartment after her last surgery to take care of her. I was feeding her. I was sharing with her all about God. We used to visit my friends. We went to church. We watched movies and ate delicious food. I took her to each doctor she needed and bought all her medicines. I served her, and I wanted to make her feel like a loved queen. She recovered her weight, she recovered her hope, and she recovered her faith. She knew she was valued and loved by her mother, her brothers, and all of us. She knew that she was deeply loved by God. She was not pale anymore; instead, her pink color returned to her face. She was recovering her beautiful smile; however, one morning when I went to her bedroom as usual, she told me she had inflammation on her leg. I asked to see but saw her leg and belly were incredibly bloated. I was terrified. She suddenly fell sick again for the third time. Four months after her second surgery, the cancer appeared again. Her belly was growing. And every day it was growing faster! In just one month and three days, she died. Her soul was saved. So she is with the best gardener. She is with Jesus Christ. He cleaned her heart and soul. He uprooted the wrong seeds in her. He allowed her to go into the presence of God. He prepared a house for her. That is a house better than she was expecting. It is in a better place than she could imagine. I believe she is more than happy in the garden of the best gardener. He is taking care of her with His love. He prepared for her and all of us a place in God's house. He has prepared a house for all of us who believe in Him.

> *"See! I am coming soon. I am bringing with Me the reward I will give to everyone for what he has done."*
>
> *—Revelation 22:12-14 (NLT)*

Jesus said He will come soon and His reward is with Him. He said that those who wash their clothes to have the right to the tree of life are blessed. Who are they? They are people who show the narrow door. However, those who live according to their flesh are in risk of losing their salvation. To illustrate the differences, I present some pictures I took in 2020 while I was writing.

The picture below shows three cases of people. The cars represent each case of those people.

Narrow gate: Holy gate

- Case 1: They are born again. Revelation 22:14 (NLV): "Those who wash their clothes clean are happy (who are washed by the blood of the Lamb). They will have the right to go into the city through the gates. They will have the right to eat the fruit of the tree of life."

Wide gate: Flesh gate

- Case 2: They are people who came back to their disordered life after being near to the narrow gate. They go for the sinful options offered by people who do not obey God: sex sins, sinful desires, wild living, greed, worshiping false gods, witchcraft, hating, fighting, unforgiveness, being jealous, being angry, arguing, false teaching, wanting something someone else has, killing other people, using strong drink, wild parties.
- Case 3: They are people who wait to see what will happen. Undecided, apathetic, unbelievers, and human wisdom. Discrimination is not my intention. I am alerting people to wake up and believe what God is showing and saying to us. He wants the salvation of everybody.

Through which door are you crossing?

"You made all the delicate, inner parts of my body and knit me together in my mother's womb. You watched me as I was being formed in utter seclusion, as I was woven together in the dark of the womb. You saw me before I was born. Every day of my life was recorded in your book. Every moment was laid out before a single day had passed."

Psalm 139: 13-16 (NLT)

This salvation includes the life of children who are in the belly of their mothers. The life is coming from God. He is who allows people to grow up inside the belly of their mother. He is our owner. He is the creator of our life. God said in Exodus 20:13 that we must not murder. So the life of a baby who is growing in his/her mother's belly must be saved.

My dear aunt loved kids, but she did not have one. That aggressive cancer made her belly grow like she was pregnant. Also, she died with her belly expanded. I remember when I was waiting for her body to be taken to the morgue, I was with my friends and her daughter. From a distance, it was highly remarkable, the immense belly. It hurt me a lot because I knew how much she loved kids but never had one of her own. My friends and I hugged and cried, and I told them: "Vanity of vanities; she never was pregnant, but she died as if she was pregnant." Like her, there are a lot of women who might want a baby but cannot. I know the story of my beloved aunt is leaving a message. Babies deserve life even when their mothers might not want them. There are families who would love them. Also, I believe that when people love God with their entire mind, their heart, and their soul, they will love everybody.

"Writing a book is like having a baby." I was told something like that by the person who mentored me. And yes, it is like a baby that we ought to love and care for from gestation. To write this book, I have been fasting, praying, crying out to God, reading the Bible and books, and even attending each place the Holy Spirit led me to. It has not been easy for me, even when I thought it would be. For most of the ideas, pictures, and structures here, I have been on my knees worshiping the Holy Spirit and asking Him for help because sometimes I thought I could not finish it. But He has confirmed to me that He is supporting what I write. He has been proving to me that it is not my flesh writing. He has been connecting one point to another and leading me through the Scriptures or books, and it is evident to me that He is supporting me. To get each topic or idea, it has been like the example of a phone connected to Wi-Fi. If I am not in the presence of God, I am not able to write because I am empty. So for me, each chapter finished has been like giving birth.

When we are writing a book, we must protect it because not everybody around you believes you have the ability to write. You might not receive encouragement from others to start and finish it. But if your book is an assignment from God, then it is in His perfect plan, and it will be led by the Holy Spirit. As a result, it will help millions of people. The same happens with a baby who is growing in your belly. If that baby is there, it is because God allowed him/her to grow in you. It is a gift from God to you that in the future, she/he might save your life and millions of others. God is our creator. So, if He is our author and our heavenly Father, my question to you is: Do you believe God creates and agrees with abortion?

Amos 1:13 KJV: "Thus said the Lord; for three transgressions of the children of Ammon, and for four, I will not turn away the punishment thereof; *because they have ripped up the women with child of Gilead,* that they might enlarge their border." Ripped up women with child was a reason for God to inflict justice in the past. What do you think will happen if abortion and killing is not stopped? Additionally, when the prophet Amos was called by God, the sins of people were: To neglect the Word of God, idolatry, pagan worship, greed, corrupt leadership, oppression of the poor, etc. So, what do you think is knocking on the door of Earth? What do you think we are living today? The Great Day of the Lord if people do not repent of their sin, or the salvation and the mercy of the Lord if people come back to God. It is in our hands and it is our decision.

> ***"Now the Lord had prepared a great fish to swallow up Jonah. And Jonah was in the belly of the fish three days and three nights."***
>
> ***Jonah 1:17 (KJV)***

Jonah was a prophet sent by God to preach against Nineveh because they were wicked and sinned a lot. God was planning to send His judgment if they did not repent. So He asked Jonah to go there. However, Jonah disobeyed Him, and he took a ship to Tarshish because he did not want to go to Nineveh. It caused a terrible storm in the middle of the sea, and the mariners were afraid. Jonah knew it was because he was disobeying God. As a result, Jonah said the crew threw him into the water. *Surprise!* A great fish was waiting to swallow him. Jonah spent three days and three nights there. I imagine it like Noah and his family in the Ark, with several kinds of animals sailing in something unusual. The turbulence, the darkness, the smell, and the noise; it was new for them. It would cause them fear. Then, the silence, the courage, the trust, the hope, the faith, and the obedience were their best gifts to inspire them to continue growing up in God. Then while Jonah was in the belly of the great fish, he prayed to God and repented of what he did. So the Lord spoke to the fish, and it vomited Jonah onto dry land (Jonah 2:10 NKJV).

Like Nineveh, currently, we can see how sin is abounding on Earth. Due to spiritual blindness, not everybody can understand what is happening to the nations. The discernment and understanding of what God is talking about are missed on Earth. The world might think everybody agrees with what some of them are doing, but there exists an awake, alert, and faithful army of God who cares about what is happening, and they are crying out to Him for help. If people do not repent of the abomination of sin, the anger of God will come. He alerts His church to talk about what is coming because He wants the salvation of everybody. However, each one decides if they believe or not.

I see Jonah inside the belly of the whale similar to The Great Day of the Lord and COVID-19. But, it is not because COVID is the judgment of God. The Word of God is not a simple book. It has His treasures that He gives to His people who spend time with Him in the secret. I can see clearly that with the story of Jonah, God was telling us the meaning of how immense His Great Day of Tribulation is. The big fish represents the Great Day of the Lord, His Anger. Jonah represents the sinner. Some people believe that COVID is the judgment of God. However, God has allowed it to happen to alert us and to send us His warning. But His Great Day does not compare with that diminutive COVID. Also, COVID confirms Daniel 12:4 NKJV which says: "Many shall run to and fro, and knowledge shall increase." Today, we know people live in a fast life without stopping. Today, we know the knowledge of man might create almost all they want. Today, we know that with the advance of technology, a war in your mind can be created with a diminutive virus that produces fear in people. It can be done with human wisdom. It is like the Babel Tower. When people want total power, they are led by the ambition of the devil, and they believe they are gods. So they believe they can build all they want, and God will not stop them. To avoid destruction and death, the world needs the wisdom coming from God.

Currently, the people disobeying and sinning without repenting are like Jonah. If they do not repent, their final destination is the anger of God and hell. The whale vomited Jonah when he repented of his disobedience, so he was saved; however, people ought to repent of sin now because God does not allow sin in His Kingdom. He vomits it out, so there is not salvation for people who do not repent before they die or the Great Day of The Lord. Even though God would like to save them, it is not possible because sin brings the consuming fire of God.

The main point with this chapter is not to scare anyone because God is love, mercy, and discipline. He is not fear. The main point here is to wake up each person who reads this book to let you know the time is coming. We are not eternally on Earth, but we have the promise of eternal life in Heaven. You have to clean your life and your heart with the blood of Jesus. The main point here is to tell you that if someone has told you that God does not forgive your sin and you are a sinner, that person has not told you the truth. God sent us His Son Jesus Christ. He cleans our sins forever, and He makes us new people when we repent forever of our sins. However, if someone has told you that with only confession, Jesus is the Lord, and this is enough to be saved, then you are on high alert. If you say you believe in Jesus Christ but you are sinning, and you have not transformed your life with the Word and presence of God, you are at risk of losing your salvation. So what do you think if you spend more time watching, reading, listening, writing, and doing what God says instead of believing what others say? Don't you think it is in our hands to receive the mercy of God instead of His anger?

CHAPTER 10

Time

"There is a special time for everything. There is a time for everything that happens under heaven. A time to plant and a time to uproot, a time to be silent and a time to speak, a time to love..."

—Ecclesiastes 3: 1, 2,7,8 NIV

For a long time, God has been teaching me how to perceive time. I might say that I move according to God's answers. In 2019, I started to graph all the main changes I have had during my life. Then I realized that those changes are about political or economic events.

Most of the time, the velocity or worry of how we live does not allow us to see those changes that are icons or milestones in us. During uncertain moments, those milestones are evident. We have to prepare for those unexpected times; the best way is to have our life built on our Rock, Jesus Christ. His wisdom allows us to understand the seasons of our life, comparing us with trees. My beloved aunt was an expert at gardening. I could understand through her job what the Scripture says about the seeds and trees.

It starts with a seed. That seed has to die, so the trees start to grow up. The seed must have good earth, water, and a gardener to grow with strong roots and give good fruits. It is the same with us. We are a seed of God. We will flourish or die, depending on our life's decisions and our obedience to God. It will depend on where we are planted, and how we are feeding our spirit. Similar to trees and their seasons, we have ours also. The closer we are to God, the less dramatic or surprising the transitional moments are because we are growing in the Rock, Jesus Christ. God wants all of us to be prosperous. He wants to give us prosperity, but that prosperity starts with our obedience, fidelity, and love for Him. It is not about money or material riches, as some people believe. It is seeking God first. Then the rest will follow. The real prosperity God wants to give us is our mind, heart, and soul. He wants to give us gifts and talents that only the Holy Spirit can give us. Then, when we transform into new men/women in Jesus Christ, we become a fertile land, and we are prosperous in everything according to God's will and plan for us. If you tell me that you do not believe in God Father, Son, and Holy Spirit, but you are prosperous, I tell you that it is a fictional and momentary prosperity because your happiness is not dependent on your material wealth. The real peace and joy is missing in you.

So, why mention this if I am talking about time? Because the time for the truth has arrived. We all have to understand that the only way a person, family, city, company, country, and the world can give good fruits and flourish is to die to our will and obey the will of God. He wants to save us from slavery and death to really give us a better life.

When we are in a deep relationship with God, He shows us what is coming and what is operating in the environment. He teaches us to perceive time. Then we can act ahead of the next thing that is coming. I have a lot of testimonies about that. One of them is with the difficult situation of Venezuela. Before the scarcity of food in Venezuela started, in January of 2016, the Holy Spirit showed me several times that I had to buy food. He led me to the scripture Genesis 41:1-4, the seven years of well-favored cows and ill cows lean flesh. In different ways I was receiving that word, so I told my mother and some friends that we had to buy food. I bought all that I could buy. Then, sometime after, the food started to disappear. However, I had bought enough for my family and me for some months. After that, the food situation there started to form part of the transition season that is living in Venezuela. It was getting worse. A lot of lines formed to buy food. However, I was calm because we had God.

Then the cash, the medicines, the gasoline, etc. started to disappear. We were one of the richest countries in oil-gas, gold, aluminium, tourism, human talent, etc.; however, when sin is leading in a person, family, city, country, or the Earth, the result is destruction. It does not matter on how much money or material riches a person or a country has to be prosperous. As I mentioned before, it is not the only prosperity God wants to give us. It depends on how much peace, joy, love, wisdom, mercy, piety, and calm exists in a person, family, or country. Then we are able to value and grow up in other areas. The external factors do not buy peace, joy, and salvation to avoid destruction. It matters how much we are near to God to be blessed, prospered, and saved. I know it will happen to my country and all places where people are humble and obedient to God and His Word.

In the middle of 2019 the Holy Spirit clearly talked to my spirit and told me that Jesus Christ is coming soon; however, as the time of Noah's Ark, people are distracted and do not believe it. Then by the end of 2019 I knew I had to write this book. As a result, what happened in 2020 was not a total surprise to me because months ago God showed me something was coming.

If you ask me again why I am talking about that, I answer that we are in the prophetic times. To perceive it, we have to spend time in the presence of God. The environment, nature, and the times have been speaking, but the distractions of the people do not allow them to understand, hear, smell, and feel what is operating. God has promises and purpose for His people, but those promises and plans have conditions and times. You have to prepare to keep firm in those promises despite what you see or how much you have to wait. A lot of sermons, books, motivational events, positivist thinking, false doctrines, etc., mention amazing and blessed gifts of the universe or even promises of God, but an important piece is missing. The path, time, faith, attitude, gratitude, obedience, love, mercy, piety, forgiveness, and honor the we need in order to wait and keep focused with our eyes, minds, hearts, and souls in the love of God. We have to believe and honor the power of what Jesus Christ did on the cross. We have to grow up with the Holy Spirit; otherwise, we will fail during the wait.

> *Jesus answered and said to scribes and Pharisees: "An evil and adulterous generation seeks after a sign, and no sign will be given to it except the sign of the prophet Jonah."*
>
> *—Matthew 12:39*

Even when some people would like to simulate or say the day when Jesus Christ is coming again, nobody knows the exact day and hour it will happen; however, He commanded that we must pray every time. It is written in Matthew 25:13.

On December 31, 2019, my family, some friends, and I were praying in my mother's house. In the middle of my prayer, I was praying about the importance of Jesus Christ in our lives. I was talking about the importance of being in His presence because He wants to have dinner with us, and He stands at the door knocking. Then a few seconds after I said that, someone started insistently knocking on the door of my mother's house. It was my cousin with a traditional Venezuelan Christmas food plate full of delicious food. God always talks; we must understand what He is telling us. It is time to listen to what God is telling us. It is time to leave the old life of loving God with our mouths and to start to love Him with all our minds, hearts, and souls. It is time to pray at home and everywhere with our family and friends.

> *"Close up the windows, bring the sun to my room through the door you've opened. Close inside of me the light you see that you met in the darkness."*
>
> *—Lyric from "Time to Say Goodbye"*

When I was working in Angola, I was in a WhatsApp group with some Venezuelan friends. It was called "good music." We sent good messages, music, and experiences. I remember the first song I sent was "Time to Say Goodbye" by Andrea Bocelli and Sarah Brightman. I felt in my heart that a new life was coming to me. I had forgotten that song, but when I quit the company and I told the group, one of my friends recalled that it was the first song I had sent to the group. When we receive the call of God and we want to know more about Him, our life and actions start to hear what God is saying in our hearts. Since early in my life, God taught me to say goodbye to things. Then, He showed me how to say goodbye to places and peoples. This does not mean it does not hurt, but we have to do what God asks. It deeply hurt, but God helps us to do it. We have to say goodbye to everything when we really want to follow His plan for us in our life, instead of our own plans.

We must cut with ties or other things that might want to keep us in the same place. When I know I have to say goodbye to something or someone, I start to prepare to set free what I have to. Most of the time, you have to do it with people or things that you love with all your heart because God asks us. We might not be prepared, but we have to trust Him. It might look like we are leaving our beloved people, but the plan of God in our life is to include more people in His plan.

This year in 2020, my lovely aunt Dai will have left three years ago to the presence of God. Still, I miss her a lot, as well as Abuelita. For some reason sometimes I believe they are in Abuelita's house, but then I realize that they left. With Mamá, my other grandmother, time and Jesus Christ have helped me, but also I remember and miss her sometimes. When I said goodbye to my two grandmothers, it was because I had to travel. With Mamá, the reason was for work, and with Abuelita it was because I had to come to the U.S.A. With them both, I did not imagine it was my last time I would see them alive. With Dai, I had to say goodbye because God said I had to give her to Him. I did it; however, I had faith she would live.

It was hard and painful to have that conversation with her. I was telling her how much we loved her and thanked her for all she did with us, but at the same time, I was setting her free for God. It was almost 5:00 a.m. Dai had not slept at all; I could hear her from my bedroom. She had gone two weeks without sleeping well. She was in a lot of pain. I woke up before 5:00 a.m. and I started to pray, and I was crying for her. I was not sleeping also because I could hear her suffering each night. When I was praying, the Holy Spirit reminded me of when she used to give me Bs 100 every month for me to buy food or transportation to the university. It was not a lot, but it helped me. So,

I thanked God for giving her to me as my aunt. I thanked Him for all she did for me and my siblings with her love. I told Him to forgive me because I was trying to retain her with my faith, but she was suffering, and I did not want her to suffer. I told Him she was from Him. Then I went to her bedroom. I sat at her bed to talk with her. It was my first time crying in front of her since she was sick because I used to do it in my bathroom to avoid her hearing me. I did not want to make her suffer for me. Sometimes even I could not see her face because I just wanted to cry. I started to thank her for all her love for us, and for all she did for me. I told her: "Thank you for each vacation you gave us. Thank you for the beautiful clothes you bought for us when we were children. Thank you for all that you taught me when I was a child and a teenager. Thank you for the Bs 100 you gave me each month when I was studying at the university. Thank you for loving us a lot. I love you with all my heart. We love you with all our hearts. You are important to all of us. We all love you." While I was telling her all that, I was crying, in a silent way, but she knew I was crying. Then she told me: *"No llores mija" (Do not cry, mija).* She called me mija most of the time. "I do not want you to be sad; I am prepared to go if I have to go. I love all of you as well. Thank you for all you have been doing for me, mija. You are the daughter that I did not have." Then I went to prepare her breakfast. I was losing my strength because she did not want to eat anything. I felt that my hands were tied because I could not help her. The big belly and the pain did not allow her to eat even when she was hungry. She was a strong woman. She was a warrior. Mi amada tía. She was more than my aunt. Today, I can say: "Thank God for letting me help her to find the light to *your* presence."

> *"For my thoughts are not your thoughts, neither are your ways my ways, saith the* Lord*. For as the heavens are higher than the earth, so are my ways higher than your ways, and my thoughts than your thoughts."*
>
> *Isaiah 55:8-9 KJV*

Our thoughts are not God's thoughts. Our ways are not God's ways. Our times are not God's times. He allows some things to happen to transform them into blessings even when we do not like this. Today, we see the consequences of sin worldwide. It produces damage, destruction, and death. However, God has better thoughts for His Earth and His people.

Same as the trees and the Earth, our life has seasons. So, like trees that grow up with a seed that needs darkness, and the Earth that God created to give life and form at the beginning when it was disordered, void, and dark, I would compare this to our life. It has the beginning, transitions, and end seasons. Starting from a season of some trees, I will compare our life with real pictures of them, taken by me in 2019.

The different colors represent transitioning seasons in figure 1. I would say that transition in us starts when we are moving from the kingdom of darkness to the kingdom of God. Then we will have more transitions because, as Proverbs 4:18 KJV says, our path is as the shining light that shineth more and more unto the perfect day when we become just. Just are all people who believe in Jesus Christ. We are similar to the trees in that some change their color or lose their leaves before others during the changing season. In the pictures, we can see how some plants are amazingly green and others are showing that they will change soon. It depends on the purpose and time of each one. This also happens with us, so if we are planted in the Land of the Lord, we will complete our purpose like each tree completes their process during each season when they are planted in fertile land.

(Figure 1: Trees in transition season.)

Then Figure 2 represents the trees in the new season. They look dry or dead; however, it is not the final season of those trees. This is similar to us. Even when you think you have lost all, or you did all you could do for something, someplace, or someone but it looks like it had no value or it was not important to others, we just have to know that, to God, all we do is important. He is watching us 24 hours a day. He has the final word. So if you really have been desiring to know God, if you have the right heart with Him, if you are obeying Him but you see something similar to those trees in you, keep trusting in God because He is working on you. Jesus Christ is ordering your life, and He is fighting for you. He is ripping up all that is not from Him. He left a promise to us in Psalm 92, so believe it because what you physically or externally see is not the same as that which is spiritually happening to you. You are growing. You are creating your life on the Rock Jesus Christ. So keep trusting, keep doing, keep praying, keep worshiping, keep fasting, keep forgetting, keep forgiving, keep loving, keep believing. Psalm 92:12-15 NIV: The righteous will flourish like a palm tree, they will grow like a cedar of Lebanon; planted in the house of the Lord, they will flourish in the courts of our God. They will still bear fruit in old age, they will stay fresh and green, proclaiming, "The Lord is upright; He is my Rock, and there is no wickedness in him."

(Figure 2: Trees after the first transition time)

Chapter 10: Time

Then when we continue believing in God, we find a light in our path. This happened to me, it happened to my beloved aunt, and it happens to you. Since I knew the truth with Jesus Christ, I have been living in His peace and His love. Since I was young, I knew that The Lord is my provider. Psalm 23:1-4 NKJV says: "The Lord is my shepherd, He make me to lie down in green pastures. He leads me beside still waters. He restores my soul; He leads me in paths of righteousness for his name's sake. Even though I walk through the valley of the shadow of death, I will fear no evil for you are with me; your rod and your staff, they comfort me." Always there is a light in our way. That light is Yeshua Hamashiach, Jesus Christ the Messiah. He is our Redeemer, our Saviour, our Healer, our Teacher, our Brother, our Friend, our Guide, our Leader. Jesus said in John 8:12 NLV: "I am the Light of the world. Anyone who follows Me will not walk in darkness. He will have the Light of Life." Jesus is always waiting for us. He is the only one who opens our path to God. No one else can do that.

(Figure 3: Trees with the light)

Finally, Figure 4 shows leafy green trees. When we build our life in Jesus Christ, we become like those trees. John 15: 1-5 NKJV says: "I am the true vine, and My Father is the vinedresser. Every branch in Me that does not bear fruit He takes away; and every branch that bears fruit He prunes, that it may bear more fruit. You are already clean because of the word which I have spoken to you. Abide in Me, and I in you. As the branch cannot bear fruit of itself, unless it abides in the vine, neither can you, unless you abide in Me. I am the vine, you are the branches. He who abides in Me, and I in him, bears much fruit; for without Me you can do nothing."

(Figure 4: Trees near a river)

I realized that God has asked of me several Arks. The first was when I was in Venezuela. He told me, "Bring an Ark to your house." I did not understand, then that week I knew He was asking to open a friendship group (a group from the church to give God's Word in our houses). I did not just open my friendship group. I also started to talk about Jesus Christ to my family, friends, and each woman, man, young person, and adolescent I have the opportunity to because I always say that I want God to tell me: *"Well done, good and faithful servant; you have been faithful over a few things, I will make you ruler over many things. Enter into the joy of your Lord"* Matthew 25:23 NKJV. I guess I did well because then He asked me to write this book. He asked me for this Ark. I might say it is my Ark of conviction, the Ark of repentance, the Ark of obedience, the Ark of subjection, the Ark of holiness, the Ark of love, the Ark of hope, the Ark of faith, the Ark of forgetting, the Ark of forgiveness, the Ark of falls and rising, the Ark of service, the Ark of salvation.

We have Jesus Christ as our only solution to clean our sins and to give access to the presence of God. So when Jesus comes again, how do you believe He will find you?

Will you be doing the will of God or yours? Will you have the identity given to you by God or the identity that the lies of the world have told you? Will you be a leader like Jesus Christ? Will you be like a lush green tree bearing wonderful fruits or will you be like a dry tree without giving amazing fruits? Will you be the kind of person like the raven that went out of the Ark or will you be like the dove that came back to Noah with a fresh olive leaf in her beak?

If you want to be the kind of person like the dove and form part of the army of God, just repent of your sin and open your heart to Jesus Christ and the Holy Spirit. Then He will put in your mouth His amazing Good News of faith, hope, love, and peace to share with others.

Jesus said in Isaiah 61:1, "The Spirit of the Lord God is on me because the Lord has chosen me to bring good news to poor people. He has sent me to heal those with a sad heart. He has sent me to tell those who are being held and those in prison that they can go free."

You can be one of those people that gives salvation to others with the Truth and Good News of Jesus Christ.

Made in the USA
Columbia, SC
07 May 2024